Date Due

DEC 17			
DE 28			
JAN 11			
FEB 9			
MAR 1			
AUG 11			
OCT 15			
NOV 23			
MAY 27			
OCT 16			
JAN 13			

BRODARi, INC.   Cat. No. 23 233   Printed in U.S.A

BACK TO BLACK

BACK TO BLACK

Comic Sketches by
Arthur Black

METHUEN/CBC ENTERPRISES
Toronto   New York   London

Back to Black is published in conjunction with CBC Enterprises.

Canadian Cataloguing in Publication Data
Black, Arthur
    Back to Black

ISBN 0-458-81210-2

I. Title.

PS8553.L32B32 1987   C814'.54   C87-093936-X
PR9199.3.B58B32 1987

Many of these sketches have been broadcast over the airwaves of the CBC or have appeared in the pages of various newspapers across the land. My thanks to the Corp., to *Ontario Living* and to those newspapers for permission to have them reappear in this book.   A.B.

Design and photography by Falcom Design & Communications

Printed and bound in the United States of America
1 2 3 4   87   91 90 89 88

CONTENTS

PART 1   ERSATZ DEER AND STONEHENGE

PART 2   A MOOSE ON A HUNGER STRIKE

PART 3   STILL PUDGY AFTER ALL THESE YEARS

PART 4   HEAVY BOLOGNA BULLS SOLD WELL

PART 5   PLAID SHIRTS AND PINE TREE PANORAMAS

PART 1
ERSATZ DEER AND STONEHENGE

SWIMMING IN THE ELORA QUARRY

EVER GONE FOR a swim in a quarry? To me, it's one of the most delightful treats you can give your body. With water, anyway. There's something about the clarity of the water and the towering limestone walls that makes quarry swimming highly sensual. Especially if you deck yourself out with snorkel and face mask and dip into the beautiful world below the surface.

Or perhaps it's just a personal fetish. After all, I learned to swim in a rock quarry when I was a mere guppy, several hundred years ago. The Elora Quarry, it was . . . a magnificent crater in the landscape between the southern Ontario towns of Elora and Fergus. The Elora Quarry is—well, heck, I don't know how big it is, but it's big. Wide enough that my arms turn to spaghetti when I try to swim across. And the distance from the lip of the quarry to the dancing blue-green water far below is such that I take a deep breath before I even peer over the side. As for the daredevil teenagers who actually leap off the cliffs, even they wear sneakers to absorb the smack of their feet hitting the water. Those kids don't have to worry about touching bottom. The water in the quarry is thirty feet deep, so there's really no danger.

Providing they survive the fall.

Jumping off the side of the Elora Quarry has never been my idea of a fun pastime, and there's no need anyway. There's a gently sloping path for we lesser breeds who wish to sample the water without having a mid-air coronary.

I remember the first time I walked that path. I can still feel the sharp limestone gravel under my six-year-old feet. I remember timidly entering the water and that first, terrifying thrill when the bottom drops away and you begin to flail and you realize that you are *swimming*.

Or in my case, sinking.

Ah, but I bobbed up eventually, spluttering and choking and gasping for air, but doing a kind of frenzied, instinctive dog paddle that got my mouth above the waterline every once in a while. Before that afternoon was over, I'd even learned to thrash my way from one point to another. I was no threat to Johnny Weissmuller or Esther Williams, but I was "swimming," after a fashion.

Since that day, I've swam in quarries all over Ontario. I've also tried them in Spain and Italy and Mexico. In Mexico they're called *cenotes* and they occur naturally, but swimming in a *cenote* feels just as exquisite as it does in an Ontario rock quarry.

They were all very nice . . . but only because they reminded me of the Elora Quarry. I always dreamed that one day I would swim and snorkel there again. Last spring, after a quarter of a century's absence, I moved back to the Fergus-Elora area. The quarry I'd dreamed about is just a couple of miles down the road. Last week I went back for a swim.

I discovered, à la Rip Van Winkle, that there have been some changes. The rambling cowpath that used to lead from the highway to the quarry is gone. It's been replaced by a large, paved parking lot. There's a concession stand hawking soft drinks, french fries and hot dogs. As kids we used to pedal to the quarry on our CCMs and not see another soul all day. Now there's a toll booth and it costs a dollar fifty for adults and fifty cents for kids. There are concrete pillbox washrooms, litter buckets and conservation officers every few feet. Before I got ten paces from my car I was nailed by one of the Quarry Guardians who told me, with a Happy Face smile that the snorkel, mask and fins under my arm were *verboten*.

"Why?" I asked.

"No floating objects allowed," she smiled.

No problem, I smiled back, pointing out that my mask, snorkel and fins would, if left unattended, sink like stones. The only floating object would—hopefully—be me.

She upped the wattage on her smile and hit me with the classic Eichmann Defence, "I'm sorry, but I don't make the rules."

So there I was, standing beside my beloved Elora Quarry, surrounded by leering conservation officers determined to crush any criminal activity I might have in mind. I looked around. Sure enough, there wasn't a face mask, snorkel or swim fin to be seen. Just ghetto blasters, teeny boppers, crushed dixie cups and the acrid, bitter-sweet aroma of a Controlled Substance burning nearby.

I kept trying to conjure up that Norman Rockwellish vignette of tousel-haired, freckle-faced lads on a hot summer afternoon, dangling their feet in the water. But it was difficult. Especially with Madonna screeching "Material Girls" from a suitcase radio just off my starboard earhole.

Ah, I tell ya . . . sometimes it's tough being an old fogey.

ERSATZ DEER AND STONEHENGE

ONCE I TOOK my kids to Disneyworld in Florida. It wasn't too bad till we got on a little train for a ride through—I don't know ... one of those time warp suburbs in the land of Mickey and Donald and Goofy. Frontierland, I think it was. We chugged slowly past a lot of American historical mockups while a man with a microphone told us what we were seeing. Off in the distance, right by a painted river, stood a herd of whitetail deer. That's what the man said they were. Even fifty feet away they looked distressingly fake. Rigid, glassy-eyed, their polystyrene antlers bobbing up and down robotically in a bad imitation of browsing. They were to living deer as Howdy Doody is to Rudolf Nureyev.

Which would have been okay for the kids I suppose. Except none of the kids around me paid any attention to the deer herd. No—it was the adults! Adults were snapping pictures like paparazzi at a photo opportunity with a porn star.

I was reminded of those ersatz whitetails as I read a story out of England a while back.

You know Stonehenge—that remarkable and mysterious formation of massive rocks on Salisbury Plain? It's been standing there for thirty-five hundred years while people played guessing games about it. It's been called a religious altar, a solar calendar, a lunar observatory, an astronomical computer, and a marker buoy for extra terrestrials. Truth is, we don't know precisely what Stonehenge is or why it was built. But we do know that it's man-

5

made. That somehow, prehistoric humans quarried unthinkably huge rocks—some weighing fifty tons—then somehow dragged and hauled and pushed and levered them up to twenty miles from the quarry to erect them in complex and largely undecipherable patterns at what we call Stonehenge.

An amazing achievement—and one that has drawn tourists to the otherwise unremarkable Salisbury Plain for hundreds of years. In fact, six hundred thousand curious people visit Stonehenge every year.

And that's the problem. Too many tourists visiting Stonehenge. They've climbed and mauled and sometimes chipped away chunks of the monoliths. Some idiots have done a Kilroy Was Here with spray bombs and chalk, and even chisels. But even the passive spectators do damage. Archaeologists say the very pounding of thousands of pairs of feet on the ground around the stones threatens the future of the site.

So what to do? Restrict the number of visitors? Give them all a crash course in archaeological etiquette? Close the site entirely?

They have, believe it or not, come up with something more bizarre than that. The officials are talking of ... plasticizing Stonehenge. Honest to God. The suggestion is that they close the site entirely and erect a fiberglass replica of Stonehenge somewhere else. Right now they're looking at the possibility of setting up an imitation, exact-scale Stonehenge in a nearby safari park.

Well, I say why just move it down the road? Why not make it really convenient and relocate in downtown London close to all the big hotels? How about Hyde Park? You could call it Clone henge.

Which reminds me again of that Disneyworld deer herd I started out talking about. Guy next to me on the Frontierland train was practically screwing his Nikon into his head he was taking so many shots of the deer herd. "Where ya from?" I asked him while he was changing film. "Wisconsin," he said. "You don't have deer in Wisconsin?" I asked. "Sure we do," he said. "But they don't stay still like this in Wisconsin."

THE PIKE PROBLEM

CANADIANS ARE KNOWN AS *an affable, placid lot, and I guess for the most part it's true. But scratch a Canuck too hard and you'll get a mouthful of letters to the editor—as I discovered when I wrote this piece in a newspaper column:*

One of the great, thorny, unanswered questions about living here in the Great White North is: What to do about the snakes? I don't mean real snakes. We don't have water mocassins or cobras or black mambas. Truth to tell, aside from the extremely odd, lonely, shivering massassauga rattlesnake, we don't have much at all in the way of bona fide poisonous snakes.

Our snakes come with fins, a pair of mean, squinty little eyes, and a mouthful of razor-sharp teeth. Biologists and tourists call them northern pike. Local fishermen just call them snakes.

Or worse. I've heard a fair amount of swearing in the years I lived in the north. But only when a Northerner hooks into a northern does cussing approach symphonic dimensions. The conversation usually starts with a variation of:

"Oh &#*+! I think I've got a #@&¢%$#* snake!"

It goes downhill from there.

Northern pike are the Outlaw Bikers of our waterways. They loiter in the reeds, beating up on smaller, weaker species (although never messing with those truly awesome denizens, the muskies). Despite their impressive size, their Charles Bronson eyes, and a mouthful of snaggle teeth, the northern pike is mostly bluff.

7

As fighters, they show all the spunk of a rubber boot; as a meal, they're about as enchanting as a dish of raw porcupine. Pike are full of bones. They don't call them snakes for nothing.

My learned fishiatrist friend and colleague, Dr. Skinner, has applied himself to the pike problem for years. Indeed, the Doctor has come up with a recipe for pickled pike that is flat-out delicious. But only a person with the scientific and philosophical determination of Doc Skinner could be bothered. From the time he eats your bait, through the time you're picking bones out of your tongue at the dinner table, the northern pike is just too much trouble.

Until now, that is. I bring news of a scientific breakthrough so recent I doubt that even Doc Skinner has heard of it. It's a proposal for dealing with the northern pike problem. We've tried just about everything else, so why not turn them into leather?

Leather?

Yep, leather. There's a company in Vancouver called (appropriately enough) the Mermaid Leather Company. They've been tanning fish skins for the past few years, and they've come up with a recipe which, according to Mermaid president, Bill Magee "converts a fish skin, which is very strong in itself, into a very durable material. ... We have had it tested, and it rivals cowhide for tensile strength."

Mermaid has already made leather from the skin of Pacific salmon, Atlantic cod, pollock, catfish, and northern pike from Manitoba.

The only difference between a Manitoba pike and an Ontario pike is that the latter has no idea who Ed Schreyer is.

We could have a viable industry here—fish tanning. I'm not saying it would turn Northern Ontario into an industrial juggernaut, but at least it would give us something to do with our pike.

The question is not whether we can turn pike into purses. We know that can be done. The big question is: What to call the new product? Pike skin? Nah. Sounds awful.

I've got it. Something that sounds remote and exotic and is accurate to boot. We'll call it Northern Snakeskin.

THE PIKE
PROBLEM
REVISITED

THAT WAS NOT THE *most popular opinion I've ever voiced, as I discovered in a matter of hours. My next column* read:

Ouch! Okay! Ow! I give! Look, I'm throwing down my pen! I'm coming out with my hands over my head!

If you're not one of the thousands who are trying to gun me down, rough me up or at least slap me on the wrist, then that tells me one of two things about you: you're not a fisherman and/or you didn't read my column a couple of issues back.

That's the one in which I had the temerity to say a disparaging word or three about one of the denizens of the North: the "Northern." Pike, that is. The beady-eyed, snaggle-toothed mugger that inhabits so many of our lakes and rivers. I suggested that the pike was overrated. I said he was a vandaliser of fishing lures and a despoiler of landing nets. I said that as a fighter, the pike was about as tough as Leon Spinks's grandmother.

Worse. I said that as a meal, the pike was about as appetizing as Leon Spinks's grandmother's pincushion. I suggested, in short, that the northern pike was a bad-tempered, boney, chicken-livered waste of an angler's time.

The paper carrying that column hit the street at about 2:30 in the afternoon.

The phone calls started coming in about 3 P.M.

And let us hear no more complaints about Canada Post. My mailpersons started delivering my hate mail the very next day.

Neither rain nor hail nor incomplete addresses could stay them from their appointed rounds. I got two cards addressed simply to "Stupid," care of this newspaper. Another dissenting reader simply wrote "To the Pencil-Pushing Pike Hater."

The thrust of the correspondence received so far seems to suggest, with varying degrees of vehemence, that I am ahh ... misinformed on one or two points.

First, they say, the pike is an excellent fighter. The consensus seems to be that if I thought it felt like "an old rubber boot on the line" .... chances were I'd spent too much time with the Molson family to be able to differentiate between a live fish and a dead boot.

Secondly, the folks who wrote in, insist that the pike can too provide a delicious meal. "Ever tried smoked pike?" several inquired. My answer was a shamefaced "Nope."

Other writers swore by baked pike. "The meat just falls right off the bones," they told me.

Well, I surrender. Even if I chose not to believe all the readers who phoned and wrote, I'd have trouble ignoring the news story that hit the front pages of papers right across Canada recently— the day after my anti-pike panegyric appeared.

You saw that story? About the team of Canadian chefs who walked off with the world title at the sixteenth Culinary Olympics in Frankfurt, West Germany?

You noticed what they offered as their *pièce de résistance?*

Pike mousse. No kidding.

I plan to try it myself. Right after I clean up this last helping of crow.

SEND THE
SHOES OUT
BY THEMSELVES

I HAVE NEVER BEEN A big fan of the whole concept of Extreme Exertion. For human beings, I mean. I have no quarrel with racehorses, cheetahs, peregrine falcons or Aston Martins that want to race flat out until their little piston-driven hearts burst. That is their choice. I won't stand in their way.

The same goes for joggers. I happen to believe privately that jogging is the dumbest way of spending your time this side of live grenade juggling, but that's all right. To each his own.

I prefer to stand at my living room window with something tall, cold and liver-threatening in my left hand, using my right to encourage the joggers as they lurch past my driveway. We also serve who only stand and wave.

I used to feel guilty about my hostility toward the Sweaty Sports, but less and less as time goes on. And this month alone, there have been three major developments in the field of sports that convince me that the thoroughfare marked "Sloth and Lethargy" is the only dual highway worth travelling.

The first sign was the beeping centre field fence. The Japanese (of course) have come up with a baseball fence that beeps. It's a kind of sonar system for fielders to warn them as they float back to get under a fly ball that they are in danger. As soon as they get close to the old fence: BWEEP BWEEP BWEEP BWEEP.

I suppose outfielders with depth perception problems will rush to endorse the beeping fence, but I don't see it as a giant leap forward for the game. Like the aluminum bat and artificial turf it

11

just makes the game a little more predictable and a little less human.

The second sports innovation to hit the news recently comes from Wilsons' Sporting Goods. It is the oversize tennis ball. Why would anyone want an oversize tennis ball? Because it has more wind resistance of course, which makes it travel slower. Says one player who has tried the tumescent tennis ball, "If your opponent is overpowering you, this ball cuts down his advantage."

Well, I suppose. And if the bigger ball doesn't improve your game you could always give your opponent a flesh wound in his serving arm.

Ah, but it's the third athletic breakthrough that really caught my imagination. Frankly, I'm surprised joggers got along without it until now. I refer, of course, to the revolutionary footwear soon to be available from Puma shoes—the RS Shoe—the first jogging shoe that is, as they say, computer compatible. Yep, now you can come in from your morning run, peel off your soggy sweats and just before you hop in the shower, plug your Pumas into your Apple or Commodore.

By the time you're towelling down, you'll be able to scan your very own printout, detailing how many miles you ran, how long it took you and ... how many calories you burned up doing it. Ain't progress wonderful? You bet your aerobically enhanced cardiovascular system it is.

But why stop now? Beeping baseball fences are fine, but why not go the extra step? Why not put baseballs on strings so they can't threaten outfielders' decorum by being hit out of the park? Let's play tennis with Nerf balls so everybody gets an equal chance. As for the Puma computerized jogging shoe ... hey. Why jeopardize a perfectly sound piece of technological wizardry by allowing a human foot to stomp all over it? Send the shoes out *by themselves* for your morning run. They can be programmed to come home and plug themselves in to the computer. Let's face it. If you're not *in* the shoes, slowing them down, your time can only improve.

Besides, that way you could join me at the living room window to watch your Pumas jog by while we have a couple of drinks. I'm buying.

HOW SWEET IT IS

SOMEWHERE IN THE WILDS of New Jersey, members of a group called RALPH must be just getting over one of the larger hangovers in history.

They won, you see. RALPH—which stands for the Royal Association for the Longevity and Preservation of the Honeymooners—has been trying for three decades to convince the major television networks they made a grievous mistake in yanking "The Honeymooners" off the air. Last week NBC aired a program called "The Honeymooners Reunion."

I suppose if you're not at least thirty years old, you haven't got a clue what I'm talking about. Let me explain: Back in the 50s, when the White House and 24 Sussex were presided over by avuncular old gents by the name of Ike and Louie ... when a skinny kid named Elvis was driving truck in Memphis and a skinny kid named Gretzky wasn't even born yet. Way back then, there was a TV show about a fat bus driver and his wife, and their upstairs neighbours, the Nortons. Ralph Kramden was the bus driver. Ed Norton was a sewer worker. Alice and Trixie were their wives. The whole show took place in the kitchen of the cheesiest apartment ever seen on film this side of a documentary on the Dirty 30s. Ralph was a buffoon; Norton was his foil; Alice and Trixie got to clean up the messes they made.

It was a funny show. I'd forgotten how funny until I saw the reruns on NBC last week.

The show was done absolutely live. No tape at all. So live in fact, that one night I remember seeing Jackie Gleason slip on a waxed floor and break his leg, right on prime time TV. The studio audience loved it. They applauded. Gleason looked around and gulped: "Will somebody help me outta heah?" Down comes the curtain ... a hasty little unscheduled musical interlude from the studio orchestra.

13

"The Honeymooners" wasn't usually that dramatic, but it was pretty exciting. If anyone forgot their lines, they had to improvise. If Norton cracked up Kramden and made him laugh so hard he looked like a blue serge earthquake and he couldn't get his breath —tough. We're rolling. North America's watching. Do it breathless.

Maybe that's why it was so good. Maybe that's why it's still good—in black and white even thirty years later. And this is not rose-coloured nostalgia talking here. My twelve-year-old Danny got his first glimpse of "The Honeymooners" last week. When the credits rolled he wanted to know if it was going to be on again next week.

Well, the answer is no. Not next week. But soon. Apparently some sixty-seven misplaced Honeymooners episodes were recently unearthed from somebody's celluloid cemetery. Technicians are dusting them off, sprucing them up and doing whatever it is that technicians have to do to make thirty-year-old TV film, palatable to modern television equipment. Soon to appear, they promise, on network television.

The funniest part of "The Honeymooners Reunion" (funny odd, not funny ha-ha) was the fact that the show was hosted by Jackie Gleason and Audrey Meadows. Ralph and Alice, thirty years on. And the thing is, thirty years later, they were . . . not very good. Audrey Meadows read her lines off the teleprompter as if the words were slowly rolling by, on the side of distant boxcars. Jackie Gleason looked like a benign Jabba The Hut—expensive threads, coiffed hair, a pencil-line moustache. To switch back and forth between Jackie Gleason in a bus drivers' uniform to Jackie Gleason dressed like a Miami pizza tycoon was . . . jarring to say the least.

Ah, but those are minor quibbles. The point is "The Honeymooners"—the originals—are coming back to the tube. Soon. If you're under thirty, tune in and find out what your parents laughed at. If you're long enough in the tooth to remember "The Honeymooners" . . . pour yourself a brace of Reggie Van Gleason the Third Martinis, lounge back in your silk smoking jacket, and bathe yourself in the words of the Great One himself:

"MMMMmmmmm How Sweet It Is!"

IN PRAISE
OF BIKES

IMAGINE ... NO AUTOMOBILES. Imagine you are at a meeting of city council. Picture a fast-talking promoter in a fluorescent green sports coat addressing the council, saying: "GOOD PEOPLE OF RIVER CITY, HAVE I GOT A VEEHI-CLE FOR YOU! IT WEIGHS TWO TONS, TAKES UP THE SPACE OF A GUEST ROOM. IT RUSTS, BREAKS DOWN, GUZZLES FOSSIL FUELS LIKE A WINO IN A PUNCH BOWL, LIKES TO RUN INTO BUILDINGS, BRIDGE ABUT-MENTS, TELEPHONE POLES, PEDESTRIANS AND OTH-ERS OF ITS OWN KIND ... COSTS ANYWHERE FROM FIVE TO THIRTY-FIVE GRAND NEW ... AND ISN'T WORTH DIDDLEY SQUAT ON A TRADE IN! OH YEAH ... AND IT'LL COST YA SEVERAL HUNDRED INSURANCE BUCKS A YEAR JUST TO SIT IN THE DRIVER'S SEAT. I CALL IT THE CAR! WHADDYJA SAY, GOOD PEOPLE?"

You would have the bozo committed, no? And yet that's a pretty fair description of the automobile. That's the trouble with cars—we're so used to them we have trouble seeing how absurd they've become—at least as a means of getting around in our cities.

Not so with the bicycle. As a serious alternative form of urban transportation, the bike is a relative newcomer. Which means it's okay to badmouth it. Chic, even.

The rap is that they're dangerous. That the riders take over the sidewalks, don't signal turns, don't stop on the red and generally flout the law in a most un-Canadian manner. The complaints come, primarily, from downtown car drivers who would dearly love to flout a law or two—but can't. Because they're gridlocked. Fused into a miles-long, inner-city daisy chain of chrome, steel and PVC, in what some anonymous, masochistic wag was pleased to dub "the rush hour."

And while they sit there, the drivers, fuming, white-knuckled, ulcers ticking . . . here comes this two-wheeling popinjay, flitting like a butterfly through a buffalo wallow! He is riding a vehicle you can hoist with one hand, that never needs a gas pump, pollutes no air, never boils over or goes rrrrRRRRAAaaa . . . rrrRRRRaaaa . . . with a price tag lower than the replacement cost of that right front fender where the rust is beginning to show through.

And that's bad enough. But what really hurts is the knowledge that the guy on the bike is going to get home . . . first! Leaving the car drivers behind . . . in the traffic . . . shaking fists . . . honking, perhaps.

Funny sound, a car honking. Honk! Honk!

Makes you wonder what the death rattle of the dinosaur sounded like.

BASEBALL—LIFE IN A MICROCOSM

I'M SORRY THAT WE DIDN'T have that baseball strike, a while back. Not because I hate baseball. I don't. It's all right, for a game. Used to play it myself. But that was back when baseball was called "moveups," played with Bobby Hamner's cracked bat, a softball swaddled in black friction tape to hold the stuffing in, and my older sister's fielder's mitt, if I could steal it when she wasn't looking. Back then, the rules were: four balls, you walk, three strikes, you're out; tie goes to the runner and everybody runs like hell if it goes through Bettridge's window.

Crude, but simple. And understood by *everybody*—even Old Man Bettridge. It's not like that anymore. Baseball has been mystified. It's no longer a kid's game. Now, it's a philosophical expression of life. Baseball's gone ... intangible, sort of. You know the best seller this summer? Something called *Bill James Baseball Abstract*. And it is. Abstract, I mean. It's about as exciting a read as the White Pages for Liverpool. Speaking of exciting reading, here's the lead sentence from a recent baseball column in the *Globe and Mail*: "Darryl Evans was seventeen for ninety-three (.183) although eight of his hits were home runs." All that tells me is that a guy by the name of Darryl Evans plays baseball—and I wouldn't even make book on that.

I hear otherwise rational people muttering about MVPs, RBIs and ERAs... Okay, I bribed a little kid with a quarter and found out that ERA stands for Earned Run Average. Swell. Now what does *that* mean?

17

I can't help wondering when baseball will reach the ASP—the Abstract Saturation Point. When will we finally be able to embrace the intellectual essence of baseball unencumbered by the messy reality of actual, sweaty, on-the-diamond, break-out-the-pine-tar . . . games?

Well, why not? Why can't we simply appoint a committee—or a computer—to boil up a daily pottage of pitching, hitting and fielding percentages, complete with box scores, league standings and personnel statistics? Why bring ugly, unpredictable human error into it at all?

Baseball. "A ridiculously simple game." That's what Albert Einstein called it.

"Life in a microcosm!" That's what Howard Cossell called it.

One suspects that the truth—like an infield base hit—lies somewhere in between.

THE SPORT OF FLINGS

A IN'T LIFE WONDERFUL? Just when you think you've got it all figured out and the rest of your allotted span on this planet is going to resemble a cakewalk executed by Fred Astaire, Fate drops a cosmic banana peel in your path and you end up doing a reverse cartwheel followed by a nine point pratfall.

Now you take wrestling. I've always done more than my share of sneering at wrestling. A celebration of silliness, I've called it. A sport for mouth breathers and knuckle draggers. A pathetic visual pageant for folks who found "Bowling For Dollars" and "Let's Make A Deal" too mentally taxing.

Oh yeah? So how come last Sunday evening found me juggling a stale coke and a limp hot dog, sitting in Section 90 Row D Seat Eight in the west attic of Maple Leaf Gardens in downtown Toronto?

Because sitting in Seat *Nine* etc., of the aforementioned, was Dan, the resident twelve-year-old. Dan in most respects is a normal, God-fearing, law-abiding lad. He has only one grave and crippling character defect.

The kid loves wrestling. Watches it on TV like a junkie every Saturday. Cheers his heroes, gives humongous raspberries to his villains. Believes every overacted, hammily histrionic second of it.

"Dan," we murmur to him gently, "you know that Corporal Kirshner, the Marine Commando wearing combat fatigues and paratrooper boots didn't really kick his opponent, the Iron Sheik,

19

thirty-seven times in the face, don't you? You realize that if he actually kicked him even once, the Iron Sheik would be, if not dead, at least spitting out teeth like Chiclets? Dan, what we're trying to say is, we hope you realize that wrestling is not ... well ... exactly ... *real?"*

Dan does not hear any of this. He is cheering wildly for the Iron Sheik (250 pounds) who is pretending to jump up and down on Corporal Kirshner's sternum (one point oh three eight ounces approx.).

Ah well. One thing I've decided about The Sport of Flings: it is sheerest folly to try and convince a true wrestling devotee that there is anything remotely, ahhh ... contrived about the game. It's not so much that the diehard fans actually believe that every body-slam and double suplex is for real ... it's more that they don't really *care.* Authenticity is largely irrelevant. Asking whether wrestling is fake or not is somewhat akin to asking whether jazz musicians can read musical notation or whether Punch and Judy aren't a tad too wooden.

Who cares? It's utterly beside the point. Wrestling is something like a passion play—important not so much for the calibre of the acting as for the emotional baggage it unloads on behalf of the audience. I don't think wrestling fans truly believe that those behemoths in bathing trunks are actually *fighting.* I don't think it really matters to them. What matters is that something very fundamental involving Good versus Evil is getting reaffirmed.

Or refuted.

Or whatever.

The one lesson I learned about wrestling—sitting there among seventeen thousand fanatics—was, not to be terribly analytical about it. Wrestling is neither a Zen Experience nor Waiting For The Cross Town Bus. It is somewhere in between. Personally, I would place it between winning a free book of Wintario tickets and not being the second-to-last patient in the dentist's waiting room—but that's just my twisted point of view.

All I know is I spent a smokey, ear-splitting evening in Maple Leaf Gardens watching outsized Homo sapiens with names like Brutus Beefcake, Special Delivery Jones, Cannonball Parisi, Greg The Hammer Valentine and George The Animal Steele perform elaborate if heavy-handed ballet routines with one another to the ecstatic appreciation of a coliseum full of spectators.

Call me easily impressed—hell, call me an out and out sap—I confess to a sharp intake of breath as I watched a blond hulk by the name of Hogan intercept a pinwheeling maelstrom of malevolence called Randy Macho Man Savage. What you have to understand is that Macho Man had just launched himself at the aforesaid Hulk from the very top ropes of the wrestling ring. Macho Man weighs 235 pounds. Hulk Hogan caught him in mid-air and threw him out of the ring. All of that is hard to fake, no matter how crooked or artful one might be.

Highlight of the evening? I would say when the Iron Sheik, who arrived waving an Iranian flag, got stomped by the stalwart Corporal Kirshner, who won the crowd over by flapping a good ole Canadian Maple Leaf banner through the ring.

The Corporal—true, blue-eyed and honourable—prevailed. The Sheik—swarthy, devious and vanquished—moaned and groaned.

Would that the world were that simple.

MY FAVOURITE KIND OF MUZAK

AS TIME GOES BY, one of my big problems is dealing with how fast the rest of the world is aging. Girls I used to chase are on the threshold of grandmotherhood. Rock stars I used to idolize are collecting their old age pensions.

Me? Oh, I'm still eighteen—but time sure marches on for the rest of you. Institutions, too. You know what's already well past its Golden Jubilee?

Muzak, that's what.

Yup. It was, believe it or not, way back in 1934 that a gaggle of Cleveland businessmen put together a plan to provide piped-in music for restaurants and hotels. Background music. They decided to call it Muzak.

For reasons that have never been fully explained to my satisfaction, Muzak caught on. Today, eighty million people hear Muzak every day. They hear it in elevators and department stores. They hear it on factory shop floors and while they're waiting to have root canal surgery. Heck, some farmers pipe Muzak into their chicken coops. They claim hens lay better with Muzak.

Maybe so. But does Muzak have to be so ... well ... *muzacky*? Must it be so blah and tasteless and dull and insipid and devoid of anything resembling life?

Yup, it must. That's what makes Muzak work, according to the people who produce it. They say Muzak is not *supposed* to be entertaining. Its purpose is to "increase productivity in the workplace."

And damned if it doesn't do just that.

Not cheaply, mind you. It costs about four thousand dollars for installation and two hundred dollars a month to "Muzak" one floor of an average big-city office building. Thenceforth the working days of everybody on that floor will be seamlessly segmented into fourteen-minute chunks of breezy, vaguely familiar, can't-quite-place-the-tune-but-it-sure-is-inoffensive ... *noise*.

Every fifteenth minute is devoted to silence. Then it starts all over again.

Does anybody (aside from battery farmers, cost efficiency experts and Muzak stockholders) actually *like* the stuff?

You betcha. Ninety percent of the audience love it, if the corporation's surveys are to be believed. Artist Andy Warhol was an unabashed fan. "My favourite kind of music" he purred.

Ex-U.S. President Johnson liked the stuff so much he had speakers nailed to the trees around the L.B.J. Ranch. Muzak has even been out of this world. Guess what the Apollo astronauts had to listen to between instructions from Houston Control?

Oh yes, it's everywhere. They play Muzak in the White House. You can even hear syrupy gobbets of the stuff oozing down the corridors of the *Pentagon*.

I have this recurring nightmare. It's the day after President Reagan has mistaken the "FIRE" button for a black jellybean and inadvertently started The War. The missiles have flown. Washington has been reduced to a smoking ruin of rubble and debris. The whole city is silent except for the occasional explosion of oil drums and gasoline tanks, the trickle of water from burst water mains and the moan of the wind through the tangle of downed wires.

And one other sound. It's coming from ... over there. From that huge, fortress-like ruin.

It can't be! Yes, it is.

Ferrante and Teicher.

JOGGING
ON ITS
LAST LAP

IS IT MY IMAGINATION or are there fewer joggers out on
the road these days? It's not just winter coming. Winter never
stopped real joggers before. Nope, I could be wrong but I have a
gut hunch that jogging is entering its last lap as a mass appeal
mania.

Which won't make me even a teensy bit sorry. I've always had
trouble with the very concept of jogging. My theory is that God
gave us pain as a kind of universal shorthand that means: "Quit
it." Pain means stop what you're doing and try something else.
Jogging causes a great deal of pain ... and the more you do it, the
more it hurts. Now I know that committed joggers will say that's
not true. All I can say is they haven't tried to jog with this body. I
listen to the plaintive little cries and whimpers emanating from
my lungs and calves and buns and bunions when I try to jog ...
and what they are saying to me in near-perfect, four-part har-
mony is: "Stop this nonsense and lie down right now."

Another development that convinces me that North America's
insane compulsion to run along highway shoulders sucking bus
exhaust is winding down ... is the fact that jogging is taking on
exotic variations and transmutations typical of a fad that's ter-
minally stricken. Exerlopers, for instance. Have you seen these
things? They look sort of like leaf springs from a small car and
they attach to the bottom of specially adapted sneakers. They are
dedicated to the proposition that you can get a lot more benefit
from jogging by ... not jogging. You just sort of bounce up and

24

down in one place on your exerlopers. And hope that no one sees you and reports you.

Jogging has also gone underwater. Honest. You can now buy little inflatable booties and upper arm water wings that will keep your nose above the waves while you churn out a ten-mile run or a series of hundred yard dashes in the deep end of the pool. "It's great," enthusiasts bubble, "no more worry about dogs or bike riders or breathing car exhaust!" Right. Now you just have to worry about chlorine fumes, pneumonia and drowning.

Some folks call this new underwater running "Flugel Fitness." I call it the death rattle of jogging, and I'm happy to report that in Hollywood, where all fads eventually go to die ... jogging is already terribly passé. In Hollywood, the In Thing now is ... Not Eating.

Three-martini, four-hour lunches are no more. Fashionable Hollywoodites now spend their lunch breaks taking saunas with their agents or rinsing their egos at the analyst.

Even the famous Hollywood working breakfasts have shrivelled to a shadow of their former excess. Says one movie producer: "Six years ago during my first breakfast in Hollywood, I was offered everything from omelettes and sausages to French toast. The last four breakfasts, I've had my choice of fresh fruit or juice and bran muffins or dry toast ... presented as a gesture of concern."

Of course. If you're not going to engage in life threatening pastimes like jogging to burn off calories ... then you've got to cut down on the calories coming in.

Personally, I substituted Not Eating for Jogging long ago. It's a simple matter of toting up calories and doing without something, that's all. For instance, jogging one mile, burns off about 100 calories. This means that I can achieve the equivalent of a five-mile run, simply by not eating ... a half pound of liver, say ... or two helpings of spinach. I can get the caloric benefits of running the Boston Marathon simply by not eating a wheelbarrow full of limberger cheese.

Well sure it's a sacrifice. But you don't think Arnold Schwarzenegger and I got these bodies by just sitting around, do you?

CURLING UP IN FRONT OF MY VIDEO FIRE

R EMEMBER THIS?

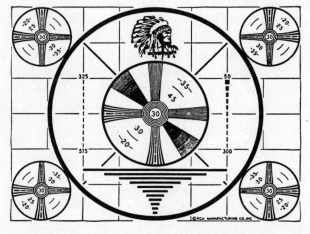

From the frontier days of Canadian television. The original test pattern. This represented about 96 percent of all TV programming on my TV back in the fifties. During those early days we only got a couple of hours of actual programs each evening. Turn on the TV any other time and what you got was an extreme closeup of a blizzard in progress.

I was reminded of this old test pattern when I tuned into my local community cable channel recently. My local channel is a lot like the early days of TV. It too, lacks programming. The folks who run it can't afford commissioned scripts or on-location shoots or ACTRA rates. After they've broadcast the Tuesday night Town Council Meeting, the Community Bulletin Board, the Junior B game with the guy who runs the Texaco station doing the play by play ... that's pretty well it for Prime Time Community Cable ... which leaves you with a lot of Zamfir flutes backgrounding lost doggie alerts ... reminders about the Over Forties' Get Fit For Spring Dancercize Classes ... that sort of thing.

Until last week. Last week I turned on my community cable channel and discovered ... fire! In a fireplace—you know—birch logs crackling away? And that was it! Stationary camera. Fire in fireplace. Hour after hour! I know! I watched! Why wouldn't I? I had the options of "Three's Company," "Wheel of Fortune," "Bowling For Dollars" or a full-colour twenty-four-inch Toshiba-vision blazing fire. Guess what I chose.

I liked the fire so much I taped it on my VCR.

I hope some modern-day Marconi scoops up this video ball and runs with it. Think of the possibilities. Beyond fire, I mean. How about an aquarium? Angel fish, neon tetras, kissing gouramis swishing around in your living room. How about sunsets? Seas-capes? What's wrong with featuring a famous painting by a master on your TV? A different one each week. Imagine turning on the set to look at ... the Mona Lisa. No pseud with a lisp to explain the significance; no vaseline-lensed retrospective about what da Vinci was going through psycho-sexually or where he bought his canvas. Just ... the Mona Lisa. Exciting!

But for me ... my evenings are pleasant enough curling up with a volume of Dickens in front of my video fire. I don't have to fret about chimney heat loss, sparks in the carpet or hernias from lugging birch logs in from the woodpile. And if the fire dies down and a chill pervades the room ... I just rewind the tape.

When you think about it, it's just as well they decided to go with test patterns instead of a video fireplace, way back when television was just starting out.

Otherwise we might never have developed "Three's Com-pany."

THE GREAT METRIC FOOTBALL CALENDAR

W ELL FINALLY, THE FOOTBALL season is finished. Yes, you're right—it is February, and yes, football used to be a phenomenon of autumn, associated with geese flapping southward, leaves turning crimson and frost dappling the pumpkins. I don't know what happened to the old plan. I figure give them a couple more seasons to get a few more games on the roster and they'll have direct stretcher service from the Superbowl to the spring training camps. That of course, applies *only* down in the States. Up here, the football season expires a lot earlier. The Grey Cup was battled over way back in mid-November for heaven sake. And what—aside from televised gridiron Armageddons piped in from south of the border—has the Canuck football fan had to cheer about since then? Well, there is the Football Calendar from the Metric Commission.

You hadn't heard? Oh my, yes. The Canadian Metric Commission—the folks who brought us windchill factors in watts per square metre; the folks who expect us to measure tire pressure in kilopascals—they've decided it's time to update the game of football. Accordingly, for a paltry ten thousand taxpayers' dollars, they have begat the great Metric Football Calendar.

You think this is the preamble to a Wayne and Shuster skit don't you? Nope. It's true. And not only does this calendar transform the Pageant of the Pigskin from yards to metres—it transforms the very tradition of calendars!

It was back in the year 45 B.C. that one Julius Caesar decreed that the calendar year should start on January the first. And for the ensuing two thousand and some years, no one's come up with a better plan. Until the Canadian Metric Football Calendar that is. It starts in September and ends in August.

Why? Well, why not, you old fuddy-duddy? As one of the many, upbeat, go-get-em-Canada slogans on the Metric Football Calendar puts it: "Metres mean progress!"

You can tell the Metric Commission got pretty excited about the idea of revamping Canadian Football. They've got a lot of rock-em-sock-em slogans like that. Such as: "A New Century—A New Measure!" Catchy, eh? And how about this one: "One hundred years to one hundred metres. Canada's Youth Measures up in Metres!" I'm not exactly certain what that means but it sure has a positive ring to it.

And you know it's a shame—when you see the kind of spirit and enthusiasm that the Metric Calendar makers have brought to football reform—it's kind of disheartening to see how limp-wristed and wishy washy the Canadian Football League is about the idea of Going Metric.

A spokesman says the CFL would never voluntarily go along with it. He thinks the Players Association might bridle at having to gain an extra thirty-three point seven inches every three downs. And that the defensive lines—normally not mathematical giants at the best of times—might have trouble lining up exactly thirty-nine point three seven inches away from their offensive opponents.

On the other hand, the Metric Commission doesn't have a history of waiting for citizens to voluntarily embrace their measurement schemes anyway. Chances are they'll just plunge ahead and metricate the CFL, ready or not.

In which case, you football fans in the audience could really use this Metric Football Calendar. Be the first on your block to know that under the new rules, the end zones are going to be nine point eight three feet shorter . . . and that the downfield tacklers must give punt receivers an extra sixteen point eight five inches when they're catching the ball.

Well come on! Write to the Commission! What else are you going to do for the next few months? God knows when the next Wayne and Shuster special is coming along. And the Argo training camp doesn't even open until May.

DRYLAND
SKIING

PASSED A FELLOW ON SKIS on my way to work this morning. You realize how unremarkable a sight that would be on most mornings? We live in the Great White North, after all. We get our share of snow (and Mexico's too). And of course, we never tire of bragging to tourists from Tulsa and other tropical spots: "Why we have ski trails right outside our back door, practically!"

Nope, it's really not that unusual to encounter a cross-country skier on your way to work in these parts . . . most mornings.

But hardly ever in *September*, when the leaves are still on the trees, the ducks and geese haven't even packed, much less left, and snow is nothing more than a nasty, unconfirmed four-letter rumour.

And another thing—this anonymous athlete shuffling and stabbing his way along the highway wasn't exactly decked out like Jackrabbit Johannsen. All he had on was a pair of jogging shorts, a tank top and a glistening body-stocking of perspiration.

Later in the day, I checked the apparition out with my pal, Al. He works in a sporting goods store and keeps me filled in on all the latest fitness trends—who's hyperventilating at what, activity-wise.

Al explained that what I'd seen was merely the latest exercise fad to hit this neck of the woods: dryland skiing. What you do, says Al, is you buy these funny little skis with wheels on them that look sort of like frontier roller skates. Then you buy two specially adapted ski poles, put one in each hand and ... go skiing.

Down the Trans-Canada, through the schoolyard, across the McDonalds parking lot, wherever. You can "dryland ski" just about anywhere, just about any time of year—providing there's little or no snow on the ground, of course.

Am I the only one who finds the whole concept of dryland skiing a little ... well, funny? I don't mean for serious athletes. If you're eyeballing a slot on the 1996 Canadian Olympic Team, well maybe you need a set of dryland skis. Buy them. More power to you. I hope you take advantage of every physiotherapeutic training aid this side of anabolic steroids. But you and I both know that's not the market dryland skis are aimed at. If it was, they'd only sell about 136 pairs world-wide—and 80 percent of those would be snapped up by hulking, hairy-chested East German brutes with names like Ingrid and Svetlana.

Nope, the folks who manufacture dryland skis have another, more lucrative herd of consumers in their sights: you and me. They want to sell us our very own dryland skis so we can get out there in our monogrammed, colour-coordinated, designer sweat suits and ski our buns off, all year round.

Well, I can't speak for you, but I can assure the dryland ski boys that I won't be biting on this one. Nosirree. It'll take more than a slick PR campaign and toothy endorsements from Wayne Gretzky to get me jumping on any Participactory Get Fit bandwagon.

Particularly when it's a fad masquerading as something else. Dryland skiing is like asking Kurt Harnett to sprint on a unicycle —or Alex Baumann to swim a few lengths in a pool filled with Rice Krispies!

Dryland skiing isn't skiing. It's pseudo-skiing. Ersatz cross-country. Fake.

Besides ... where would I store the damn things? There's no more room in the basement.

Not unless I sell my rowing machine, my rebounder and my exercise bike.

BEEN IN A RECORD STORE LATELY?

THERE'S AN OLD AXIOM that goes: "If you want to keep the conversation around the dinner table amiable, genteel and enlightening ... avoid talking about sex, politics or religion." I would add a fourth category to that—music. Oh, music is a wonderful topic if you get into it with mature, consenting adults with mutual musical tastes. But if you're with strangers and you really don't know how the lady on the far side of the chip dip feels about Glenn Gould or Miles Davis or the Sex Pistols ... then talk about something else. Anything else. A few thoughtlessly launched musical opinions from you, and you could end up *wearing* the chip dip.

The problem is compounded of course by the ear-numbing array of music that's around nowadays. Once upon a time, a long time ago the concept of music was relatively simple. Back then, sages even had the temerity to try and define music. The "food of love" one called it. "The speech of angels" opined another. Aldous Huxley said, "After silence, that which comes nearest to expressing the inexpressible is music." The philosopher Nietzsche wrote, "Without music, life would be a mistake." Of course Huxley and Nietzsche operated under a handicap: they never got to hear Liberace. Or Bob Dylan or Oscar Peterson or Bob Marley or Joey Dee in the Peppermint Lounge.

Have you been in a large record store lately? The divisions and subdivisions make an average sized book library look like a Mom and Pop Convenience store. In popular music alone there is jazz, and folk and blues and country and western. And disco, reggae, gospel, ragtime, rock, punk, new wave—just to name a few of the sub-phyla—and not to get into the hybrids and crossovers like

32

jazz fusion, country blues, folk rock and rock gospel. Then there's that whole other musical jungle—the world of operas, concertos, contatas, sonatas, suites, fugues, partitas and etceteras that make up so-called "serious" music. Silly classification. After he had finished a set, someone once asked Dizzy Gillespie if he also played serious music. Dizzy looked at the guy and said: "What do you think we were doing up there—kidding?"

But it is confusing—and as if categories weren't confusing enough . . . now the musicians are starting to blur. I hate to sound like my parents grumbling about the Beatles and the Stones . . . but it is getting hard to tell—well, hell, the boys from the girls out there. Michael Jackson looks like Diana Ross with a summer haircut and a missing glove . . . Boy George is playing both sides of the street. Heck, I'm still not sure about Tiny Tim.

Anyway, if you're as mixed up as I am, I have a news story that may console you somewhat. It's about radio station KIQQ in Los Angeles—and the programming they broadcast for one full day recently. It was pretty much your standard FM middle-of-the-road soft pop rock format. They'd play a song, the announcer would come on and say "That was Bruce Springsteen's latest . . ." and they'd cut to a commercial, then they'd play another song and the announcer would back announce with: "Cindy Lauper with her new hit single . . ." and that's the way it went all day.

Except for one thing. Radio Station KIQQ wasn't playing songs by Springsteen or Lauper or any of the other singers they said they were playing. All they played over and over, from 11 A.M. Wednesday until 10 A.M. Thursday, was one song called "State of Shock" by Michael Jackson.

For twenty-three hours! I don't know why they did that—a PR gimmick maybe . . . but do you know how many listener complaints the KIQQ station switchboard logged? Exactly . . . none. Not one.

That can only mean one of two things. Either no one in Los Angeles listens to radio station KIQQ . . . or my fuddy-duddy reactionary parents were twenty years ahead of their time again. I can hear their echo now. "He can't sing . . . you can't even understand the words . . . all these crazy songs all sound the same."

Do you suppose they might have been right all along?

33

ANYONE FOR HANGGLIDING?

I DON'T KNOW HOW you feel about sports, but I've always taken a kind of inverse personal pride in being completely chicken-hearted. I deduced very early in life that a fella could get hurt out there on those overrated playing fields. I retired from organized hockey at the age of nine, when it dawned on me that those big kids on the blue line really did intend to knock me down. I passed entirely on football when I saw that it consisted chiefly of two lines of foot soldiers trying to run over each other in cleats. As for the really brutal games—lacrosse and rugger—I couldn't even watch them, much less participate.

So while my young colleagues were trying out for things like corner linebacker and shortstop and right wing, I opted for the gentler sports, like ... dominos, stamp collecting, snooker and train spotting.

The pattern persisted through teenagerhood. When I was sixteen, anybody who was anybody had a motorcycle or was saving their paper route money to buy one. Big Harleys ... Norton Black Shadows ... dirt bikes. Anything, really, as long as it had two wheels, went fast and made a lot of noise doing it.

But not me. I stuck with my good old reliable CCM three-speed. And felt pretty smug about it too. Matter of fact, I think I've felt smug about my safe cycling addiction right up until last week, when I read a report put out by the National Electronic Injury Surveillance System. This is a group in the States that collects and collates accident reports from hospital emergency rooms across the country. They decided to focus on sports injuries to see which is the most dangerous recreational pasttime. Basketball's very high—197 basketball-related injuries per hundred thousand people. Well, that doesn't surprise me. Basketball's a fast-moving, intense sport, lots of bodies caroming around the court, lots of stress on the knees and ankles. Baseball caused even more injuries —it was the third most dangerous sport you can play according to the report. Again, no surprise. When the object of a game is to swing a club to thwock a rock-hard ball through a field full of players, chances of getting hurt are not exactly minimal. And here's football—the second most dangerous recreational activity, causing 217 injuries per hundred thousand people—that I have no trouble believing. I always thought football was a kind of recreational meatgrinder.

But what's this? The largest single source of recreational injuries in the U.S. over a twelve-month period was ... the bicycle!

Yup, according to this survey, it was more dangerous to go for a bike ride last year than it was to wrestle, work out on a trampoline, ski, surf or even play hockey.

More bike pedallers ended up in the emergency rooms of hospitals last year than quarterbacks, halfbacks, slotbacks, wingbacks and all those other crazy backs who got mashed and mangled playing football.

Scarey. Especially scarey because spring is coming. The snow will soon be disappearing ... and I've still got my CCM three speed.

Besides, I've got principles to uphold. I was born chicken-hearted and I fully intend to die in my sleep at age 103, chicken-hearted. Know anybody who'll take a well-used CCM three speed as a down payment on something safer?

Like maybe a hangglider?

FAIRYTALES ON TRIAL

T HAT OLD AMERICAN CURMUDGEON, H. L. Mencken, once defined a courtroom as: "a place where Jesus Christ and Judas Iscariot would be equals ... with the betting odds in favour of Judas."

I was thinking about Mr. Mencken as I read a news story about a circuit court trial that took place down in Madison, Wisconsin recently. The defendant was being tried in absentia, but she was found guilty of criminal trespass, damage to property, and theft.

Theft of porridge. The jury was made up of a bunch of first- and second-grade school kids. The defendant was one Goldilocks. The whole thing was an exercise to demonstrate to youngsters the full majesty of the legal system. A laudable idea I suppose ... but what really caught my eye was the defence mounted by the lawyer —all three and one-half feet of her—representing Goldilocks. The lawyer argued that there had been "a classic misunderstanding between her client and the Bear Family." Goldilocks, she said, had only entered the bears' domain because she had been chased by a swarm of bees.

Ladies and gentlemen of the jury, I submit that this is one defence attorney who does not have all that much more to learn about the legal system in North America. She's already mastered lesson number one: when in doubt, stickhandle.

I predict ripe pickings for this miniature Melvin Belli as she strides through the juicy litigational hunting grounds of Hans Christian Andersen, Lewis Carrol and the Brothers Grimm. She'll probably represent the suffering mother in *Alice in Wonderland*. Mental anguish—contributing to the delinquency of a minor (remember those card games?) and trafficking in a controlled substance (magic mushrooms). They could also sue the owner of that hole—call it an uncovered well—that Alice fell down. Hit him for every cent he's got.

What about Hansel and Gretel? Nobody's ever looked at that fable from the Witch's point of view. It would be a posthumous suit of course, the Witch finishing up as she did doing a slow burn in her own oven. But it's a cornerstone of our judicial system that you don't lose your rights just because you're dead. The way I see it, Hansel and Gretel, their heirs and dependants are wide open for a monster lawsuit on the grounds of trespass, unpaid-for lodging and, for those nibbles they took out of the gingerbread wainscotting—theft under $200. Not to mention first-degree witchslaughter of course.

Lots of potential pigeons for the plucking in folklore. The woodsman in *Little Red Riding Hood*—get him for break and entry and carrying an unregistered weapon. Cinderella could do time for impersonating royalty...

Snow White? She's tough because she's ... well, snow white. But the Seven Dwarfs? A goldmine. Kidnapping, unlawful confinement and failure to pay the minimum wage just for starters.

Oh yes. The Three Little Pigs for littering; Humpty Dumpty for loitering; Peter Pan for piloting a substandard aircraft ... the possibilities are endless. And I can't understand why the legal profession had to wait for a grade two defence attorney from Madison, Wisconsin to point the way. After all, lawyers have never been shy about peeling new plums before.

Reminds me of the story of two burglars holding a whispered conference outside a jimmied window. One burglar has just come out of the house. The other is standing watch.

"Did ja get anything?" rasps the sentry.

"Nah, nothin," says the other. "A lawyer lives here."

"Jeez, that's too bad," says the first. "Ja lose anything?"

REMEMBERING THE DRIVE-IN

COULD YOU, UH, HOLD IT down there? We'd like a moment's silence, if you don't mind ... for a passing institution. Bigger than the hula hoop. More pervasive than the Twist, the Edsel, even the TV show, "Bonanza."

Ladies and Gentlemen, it is with a tear in the eye (or a raindrop on the windshield if you prefer) that we remember the drive-in.

Drive-ins. Drive-in theatres. Passion pits. Remember? Remember the cruddy, tinny speaker hooked on the window? The between-features crush at the concession stand where you lined up, rumpled and blinking under the fluorescent glare while you waited for popcorn and red hots and large Cokes that were largely crushed ice with straws in them. Lined up and waited, but not before you'd popped into the washroom to check yourself for messed up hair and lipstick smears.

My, they used to be something, though. Remember sneaking in, in the trunk of a friend's car when you didn't have the price of admission? Recall the weasely little cruds with flashlights who used to pad around on crepe soles, investigating the cars where no heads were showing? Drive-ins even managed to span the generation gap. After the hormones died down the teenagers who became the young marrieds still went to the drive-ins ... their young kids in pajamas, and a picnic hamper full of snacks. The drive-ins accommodated with kiddy attraction slides and merry-go-rounds. Some of them even provided grills for cookouts and barbecues.

Well, the bad news is they're dying, the drive-ins. Folding all over the place. Oh, there are a few healthy ones left here and there. But drive-ins are not the phenomenon they once were ...

back in the fifties and sixties. It figures, when you think about it. Drive-ins thrived when land was cheap and taxes were low. Gas was cheap then as well and the automobile was king ... and big was not only beautiful ... it felt good, too.

It's one kind of experience to sit through a double feature in an Oldsmobile 98 four-door with plush power seats and enough headroom to accommodate a team of Romanian aerialists. It's something else again to watch a twin bill in a Rabbit or a Honda Civic. Not impossible ... just less majestic.

In its prime, the drive-in was a place you went to escape the heat of a summer night. Air conditioning has pretty well taken care of that. As for entertainment, well, a VHS or a Betamax will deliver the same film to your living room, where you can eat homemade popcorn, forget about trying to see past the wind-shield wipers ... and still scratch where it itches.

All of which has put the drive-ins in serious trouble. One former owner calls drive-ins the "buggy whip of the eighties." Another fellow, whose company owns fifty drive-ins down in the States, predicts they will be utterly extinct within the next few years. He's selling off and converting his drive-ins to other uses as fast as he can.

Extinct is the word, I guess. Just like the Hupmobile and the Hula Hoop. Drive-ins lasted a little longer than both of them ... been around for fifty-one years now. Fellow by the name of Richard Hollingshead Jr. opened the first one in Camden, New Jersey back in the spring of 1933. Showing a film called *Wife Beware*.

Don't know how much longer they'll be around ... but I hope at least one drive-in somewhere escapes the wrecker's ball or the paving machines or the attentions of shopping mall developers. I'd like to think that at least one drive-in would be overlooked. Preserved to perplex and bewilder some archeologist in an age to come. What would they make of a drive-in? That strange curving wedge of blank screen? That concrete bunker in the middle of a field of steel posts with primitive communication devices hanging on them. What would those archeologists think they'd discovered?

A shrine?

Well ... I guess that'd be close enough.

HOW'S YOUR LUCK?

H OW'S YOUR LUCK? Good? Bad? Average? Mine's about average, I think. I've never won a lottery or a trip for two around the world or a brand new station wagon. On the other hand I did win a pair of ski boots once as a door prize, and whenever I'm in Toronto or Montreal and I take the subway, the train stops with an escalator right in front of me an uncanny number of times.

That's about as good as my luck gets ... and that's okay with me. But I got to thinking about luck, and some people's lack of it, and other people's oversupply, after I read a story out of Atlantic City, New Jersey. Atlantic City is a big gambling spa of course. Lots of casinos, and Antonina Oliveri is a denizen of the place. She's one of those slot machine ladies. You know, the ones who show up at the casinos with a canvas bag full of silver dollars and a glove on one hand so they don't get blisters from pulling on the one-armed bandits? Well Antonina's one of those. She plays and plays, and when she runs out, she disappears for a few days. Sooner or later, she shuffles back into the fluorescent glare of the casino again, listing heavily to port under the weight of another bagful of silver dollars. And off she goes to feed the machines. She's never hit the jackpot. You could say that Antonina Oliveri doesn't have a whole lot of luck.

Certainly not compared to Bill Robinson. Bill runs a tavern in a town near Atlantic City ... and he can take gambling, or he can leave it. Last month he was walking by the bank of slot machines at Harrahs Marina Casino in Atlantic City when he decided to blow a few dollars. Well you know how seductive those things can be. Before he knew it, he was down twenty dollars. Twenty bucks! For a machine! Forget it. Okay, one more ... his last silver dollar and that's it.

On his twenty-first try, Bill Robinson won $1,236,319.10. He hit the jackpot. The casino owners decided they would get some publicity photos. So the next day, they escorted Bill Robinson, Atlantic City's newest millionaire down to the slot machine on which he'd hit the jackpot, at which they found Antonina Oliveri, hunkered down and playing intently. Well, casino owners, photographers and Bill waited patiently for a few minutes. Antonina just kept feeding the machine. Ka chunk ... whirrrrrr ... nothing ... ka chunk whirrrrrr ... nothing. Finally one of the casino people coughed politely, touched her elbow and asked Antonina if she'd mind moving to another machine ... just for a few minutes so they could take a couple of pictures. Antonina moved. They got Bill Robinson in front of the machine. Okay now, Bill, could ya just soahta pertend youah playing the machine ... Oh ya gotta dolla theyah? Super ... sure just put it in ... great hold it ... now pull the lever deah. ...

Ka chunk ... whirrr ... BING BING BING flashing lights, buzzers ... sirens. Bill Robinson had done it again! Hit the jackpot. Although it's a mere ten thousand dollars this time.

And off to the side ... Antonina Oliveri, veteran slot player ... long-time loser ... watches it all ... and hits the roof. She rears up and says "Hey ... I woulda won that jackpot if ya hadn't made me move!"

Well the good news is that the casino owners, out of fear of bad publicity or—let's be generous—from a sense of fair play, decided that Antonina Oliveri had a point. So they issued two cheques, each for ten thousand dollars—one went to Bill Robinson; the other to Antonina Oliveri.

And the really good news is that Antonina did not get her cheque converted into silver dollars. She says she'll use it to pay off her mortgage instead.

Could be that Antonina Oliveri's luck has just taken a turn for the better.

WHEN THE EAST WIND BLOWS, THE FISH WON'T BITE

When the East Wind blows, the fish won't bite.
South Wind they bite least
West Wind blow de bait right in their mouth
North Wind they bite best.

THAT'S THE GOSPEL according to Joe Lavally, a legendary Cree fishing guide who worked the Algonquin Park area of Ontario years ago. Lousy poetry ... but great fishing lore. You know why? Because it takes a stand on the whole mind-boggling problem of catching fish, that's why. Joe's little Petrarchan sonnet tells you, "Do this: you'll catch your limit. Do that: and it's warm beer and Spam from the can tonight." Fishermen love absolutes— there are so few of them in the fishing game. Someone once defined fishing as: a jerk at one end of a line waiting for a jerk at the other. Good ... but not the whole story. You have to look at Jerk Relativity.

Now you will hear talk among fisherfolk, of the wily old pike ... the clever largemouth ... the cunning muskie. Bunk. Fish are dumb. We are talking about a species that literally does not have enough sense to come in out of very heavy rain. Biologists—who are so much smarter than fish that they eat with forks, tie their own shoelaces and handle pocket calculators—biologists have determined that 10 percent of a fish's life is pure and utter Lent. Doesn't eat a thing. Five to ten percent of a fish's life is a Roman orgy with fins ... he'll eat doorknobs. That means that 80 to 85 percent of the fish you encounter will be in their "neutral phase." They're saying, "Well I really couldn't eat a thing ... but what can you show me?"

Which brings us to this, and this, and this. Fishing lures. And spinners and flies and spoons and plugs. You can buy flashing, winking, bobbing and diving lures. You can purchase lures that glow in the dark; sonar lures that send out Nelson Eddy/Jeannette MacDonald I-Am-Calling-Yoooooou sounds. You can buy lures that smell like a sardine in heat. Whatever that smells like. All designed to bring the two aforementioned jerks together. A lot of people want to know—but do they work, these lures?

Hah. All I can do is repeat the words of Joe Lavally.

> *When the East Wind blows, the fish won't bite*
> *South Wind they bite least*
> *West Wind blow de bait right in their mouth*
> *North Wind they bite best.*

That's a rule that always applies, by the way. A fishing absolute.

Unless your fishing for suckers. Suckers are different. They will bite anytime at anything. The more gaudy and outlandish the better.

Particularly if you're trolling in the shadow of the fishing lure display at the hardware store.

PART 2
A MOOSE ON A HUNGER STRIKE

SNUDOLOGY

AT THE RISK OF HAVING this slim volume thrown with unbecoming vehemence across the room . . . I have a confession to make.

I hope it snows.

Just one more time, Lord! Then I promise to sit back and let what passes for spring in these parts wash over me. But I would like one last moderately heavy snowfall—six inches, say—before the robins and nudists and Winnebagoes take over.

It's my snud quotient, you see. It is seriously depleted. Snud? Oh that's just a combination of snow and mud. It's that crud that builds up on your car fenders right behind the wheel wells. During winter, I mean—and only under the right conditions. If it's forty below or forty above, snud buildups range from pitiful to non-existent. Optimum snud-growing conditions occur right around the freezing mark, when there are a few inches of thick, soft, fluffy snow on the ground.

If your stars are in the correct configuration and you've been living a good, true, just and moral life—but mostly if you're lucky as hell—such a snud incubation situation will be followed by a quick freeze. That will render the snuds on your car rock hard.

For a snud connoisseur that's like discovering a bottle of Dom Perignon '54 in the remainders bin at the LCBO.

There are few sensual pleasures in life (well, in Northern life, anyway) to compare with snud-kicking. I mean when you go up to, say, your left front fender, discover a beautifully formed, prime

46

condition snud—a twenty pounder maybe—and then, with one well-placed kick of your bush boot, you send that snud scuttering along the roadway.

Mind you, there are hazards. Sometimes those snuds really *are* rock hard—and virtually welded to the car frame. Which explains, I think, the rise in bruised bunions and fractured toes reported by our hospital emergency wards each winter.

Then too, there's the treacherous soft snud. You wind up to do a Zenon Andrusyshyn from the forty-yard line ... really get your boot into it, only to discover that your snud has the consistency of room temperature chocolate mousse. More foot injuries. Not to mention auto body work.

Several snud afficionados have written to me asking about the classic dilemma of snud protocol. Simply put: is it okay to kick the snuds off somebody else's car?

This is an exasperatingly grey area of snudology. I don't think you can make a hard and fast rule about it. It's really a judgement call that depends on the circumstances.

As for me, I try to restrict myself to snud-kicking on my own vehicle, plus those of a few close friends. But I confess that I have, in the past, usually after a couple of drinks, kicked the snuds off strange cars late at night on deserted streets.

I make it an iron rule *never* to molest snuds on Harley Davidsons or on half-ton pickups featuring rifle racks.

Anyway, it's almost spring and the snud-kicking season is pretty well over for the year. But a guy can dream, right? Let's both dream.

Think snud.

AHHHH, AUTUMN!

Along the line of smoky hills
The crimson forest stands.
And all the day the blue jay calls
Throughout the autumn lands.

A CANADIAN POET BY THE name of William Campbell penned those observations nearly a century ago, standing— I would wager my copy of *Colombo's Canadian Quotations*—on a southern Ontario hillock, squinting off at the horizon. The lines were first drummed into my unwilling skull in a high school English class, twenty years ago. That's where they lodged, only to bubble forth spontaneously just a few days back. I'd forgotten I ever knew them until I looked at a calendar, noticed September a-looming, and realized that for the first time in too many years, I was on the threshold of enjoying crimson forests again.

My last ten Autumns you see, were spent in Thunder Bay, up on the snout of Lake Superior. They don't do crimson forests up there. Jade, definitely. Also emerald, olive, ochre—and when the birches get cooking, some quite shocking and saucy yellows and golds ... but, due to a shortage of maple trees, precious little in the crimson line.

Well, I'm living in Southern Ontario now, land of the crimson forest—and I can hardly wait for the leaves to turn. I feel like a little kid three days before Christmas. Just contemplating the coming colour changes conjures up marvellous memories. Half-forgotten, near-tribal reveries of endless, warm fall days, the scrunch of parchment-textured leaves underfoot, the smell of them burning at dusk. (I know, I know ... there are by-laws making that illegal now. But there was a time, my children...)

On Saturday mornings, scrupulously ducking the seigneurial gaze of parents, we kids would toil like worker ants to gather leaves in armfuls and plonk them in burgeoning piles. Great, spongy yurts of mouldering foliage we created. Pungent mounds that we could burrow under, dive into or plough through, Evel Knievel-style on our CCMs and Schwinns. We had as well, an added frisson of danger: our mothers' voices ringing in our ears concerning the inherent hazard of our chosen pasttime: "Don't play in the leaves! Drivers can't see you! You'll be hit by the milk truck!" Ah yes, one of the great folk myths of pre-pubescence— concerning the luckless child who disobeyed his mother, played in the leaves and got flattened by a passing motorist for his sins. I supposed it happened from time to time. Probably about as frequently as kids got stomach cramps and drowned—divine retribution for jumping in the lake an hour and forty-five minutes after lunch, instead of waiting the regulation two hours.

But I digress. Ruminating about Autumn will do that to you. It's a great, fat horse-chestnut of a cliché I know, but I'll say it anyway: Autumn is the grandest season we've got. Summer is lovely, Spring is delightful, even Winter is ... bracing, taken in moderation. But Autumn? Ah, Autumn is the fairest of them all.

When you get right down to it, we're blessedly lucky to have all four of them—the seasons, I mean. There are poor, benighted, two-legged denizens of this planet who wouldn't know maple leaves from pipe dottle; who think that snow is an exotic form of vegetation restricted to mountaintops and polar caps.

Worse still, there are whole regions of the globe in which you can't tell what season it is. Where the only way to mark the debutante splendour of Spring or the mellow *glissade* of Summer into Autumn is to take a magic marker and circle the date of the equinox on your calendar. In the Caribbean, the leaves are eternally green. In much of Europe and Asia, the only difference between the middle of summer and the dead of winter is a slight rise in the number of head colds per capita.

But here in Ontario? No way, Nanook. Lotus eaters in our West Coast rain forests may have the temerity to tease the Weather Gods; Bluenosers may get to spend 365 days a year wearing

oilskins and a Sou'wester, but here in the sometimes icy, sometimes steamy heartland, we observe the seasons. We not only
observe them, we kowtow to them like indentured vassals. We
obey because we know to do otherwise is to flirt with chilblains or
sunburn.

Except during Autumn. Autumn is such a well-bred, unthreat-
ening season, poised like a referee between its brawling siblings,
torrid Summer and withering Winter. Autumn is sensible too—
not like its batty sister of the opposite calendar quarter, sweet,
silly Spring, with all that rising sap and buzzing bees and twitter-
ing birds ... no. Autumn is also ... handy. As handy as—well, as
Lady Chatterley's gamekeeper—a polite, knowledgeable and def-
erential family retainer, respectfully tapping us on the shoulder to
remind us that soon, very soon, the indolence and lassitude we've
cultivated over a long and torpid summer will be ... inappropri-
ate.

Autumn wants to bring to our attention that, just a couple of
counties away and moving fast is a malevolent-looking, frosty-
thatched thug with blood in his eye and a broadsword-sized icicle
in his belt. He's a mean drunk called Winter and he's heading our
way. Now would perhaps be a good time to check the insulation in
the attic and make a final sweep of the garden.

Autumn. He's the well-dressed gent who this very moment is
discreetly tapping a velvet-gloved knuckle on the front door.
Clucking at our still-screened windows, tut-tutting at the uncoiled
garden hose, running an experienced thumb along the worn
weatherstripping at the back door...

*Isn't this the homeowner whose pipes froze three times last
winter? Who phoned the police last November about the thieves
who'd stolen his lawnmower, then spotted it four months later,
winking rustily back at him out of a melting snowdrift in his own
backyard?*

Ah well. You know that Autumn is much too refined to smirk
or sneer. Such a sane and civilized season it is! An English writer
by the name of Richard Le Gallienne dubbed it: "the third act of
the eternal play."

To which an admiring Ontarian, trudging through the prologue
of his own Act Three, can only clap a pair of middle-aged palms
together and cry: "Curtain up!"

FEALTY FROM A FELINE?

DO YOU HAVE A CAT? Then you have my sympathies.
Don't get me wrong. I like cats. I have one myself as a matter of fact. Actually, that statement is laughable. Nobody *has* a cat. Cats occasionally deign to let some benighted human wretch lavish free room and board on them. Cats will, from time to time, condescend to let a mere human hand stroke and fondle them. But nobody owns a cat. The very idea of fealty from a feline is ridiculous.

In his book *Animal Farm*, George Orwell wrote: "All animals are equal, but some are more equal than others." He was supposed to be writing about pigs, but I have a hunch he was actually ghostwriting a manifesto for a cadre of sly tabbies.

I'm convinced that all cats—from Siamese to alley—take it absolutely for granted that they are superior creatures, cursed by an indifferent Fate to live on the same planet with humans.

Cats care not a fig for the comfort or convenience of their (it is to laugh) masters. I once shared a house with a pregnant female cat. As her time approached her belly bloomed and I fussed around like a midwife, making sure she had a healthy adequate diet, and clearing out my hall cupboard, installing a sturdy cardboard box with lots of maternity-type blankets. "What a perfect place to have her kittens!" I hummed to myself.

She chose to have her litter at three o'clock one winter morning as I snored in bed with my arm outstretched. I was awakened by the sound of five distinct, high-pitched mewings emanating from just below my left armpit.

Mother and children got the double bed. I spent the rest of the night on the floor.

Don't misunderstand. The fact that a 180-pound member of the dominant species on the planet was booted out of his own nest by a five-pound ball of supercilious fur—that's not the point. The point is, everyone to whom I told the story—even people who didn't own a cat—just smiled and nodded as if it was the most natural thing in the world. Nobody laughed at me and called me a sentimental idiot. They all accepted without question that a cat could do that to a human.

What got me ruminating on the subject of cats was an item in the newspaper. It's about a Toronto lady, Barbara Wilson, who wondered if perhaps she was going crazy.

Every morning Barbara would be awakened by the sound of her television. It was going full blast.

She got a little paranoid about it. Last thing every night, she would check and double check to make sure the TV was off. First thing next morning, she'd hear "Good Morning America" or "Canada AM" blaring away in the living room.

She called in an electrician. He found nothing amiss. She called the cable company which had recently hooked up the television with a converter and remote control attachments. They sent out a repairman who said the system was all in order.

Last Saturday, it happened again. Barbara Wilson woke up to hear her television blaring away. This time she got up quietly, tiptoed to the living room and. . .

And found Tobi, her cat, reclining in a rocking chair, watching cartoons.

Directly under Tobi's left front paw was the remote control button.

Personally, I'm not surprised. If Tobi was really on the ball, he'd have arranged to have a bowl of Tuna Chip Dip under his right paw.

MERCHANDIZING MOSQUITOES

YOU KNOW WHAT THIS country needs? What this country needs is a shtick. A routine. A product.

All God's top-of-the-line countries got shticks. France does cuisine and haut couture. Britain specializes in fish and chips and royal tours. Italy exports tenors. America does Hollywood movies, diet books and spoiled millionaire tennis brats. And Canada? What's Canada's shtick? What do we turn out that the rest of the world lines up for? We haven't moved an ornamental Mountie since Nelson Eddy and Sergeant Preston. Furs? Hah. Brigitte Bardot took care of that. What's left—hockey players? Nope. Nowadays they mostly come with names like Lars and Sven and Vladimir from places like Helsinki and Oslo and Smolensk.

We used to get pretty good play in the lumberjack and plumber game—you know, hewers of wood, drawers of water. But environmentalists tell us that our forests are pretty well hewed out—the last box of Kleenex is in sight. As for water, well Uncle Sam is talking pipelines and watershed diversions now. The big time. Bucket brigades with a penchant for punctuating their sentences with "Eh?" need not apply.

And that's about it for Canada shtick-wise. Except for one overlooked commodity.

Bugs. We've got bugs, folks. And I'm not talking earwigs or midges or cabbage butterflies or cutsie-poo caterpillars in Disneyworld racing stripes. I am talking man-eaters. I mean bushwhacking, backbiting down and dirty Viet Cong style alley fighter bugs. They range from the massive B-29 style deer flies and horse flies all the way down to the ephemeral but fearless and habitually blood-starved black fly. But the pride of the fleet is the one that comes in somewhere in the middle, size-wise, and thrives everywhere from far above the treeline all the way to Rosedale bedrooms. The mosquito. Mosquito. Such a pretty name. Spanish, you know. It means little fly. Gotta wonder about the Spanish. Getting something like that wrong. It's no wonder they lost their empire.

But I'm getting off track. I don't want to philosophize about mosquitos—I wanna export them. I know they've got the critters in Europe and in the States and other places, but not like Canadian mosquitos. Not ones that make you fear to leave household pets and small children untethered in the backyard. Not ones that you can stuff and mount and hang on the rec room wall. No, Canadian mosquitos are in a class by themselves. And we can sell them! All it would take is a little promotion! What's the matter? You don't think Canadian mosquitos would get good play in Peoria? You don't think TV watchers would tune in to watch celebrity sportsmen toting Remington pump actions throwing down on a covey of incoming mosquitos at twelve o'clock high? You don't think *Field and Stream*, *Saga* and *Sports Afield* would send their best staffers out to write features on trophy bughunting? wing shooting the Yukon bloodsucker? or first-person narratives with titles like: "I Went Mano a Mano with the Vampire Bugs of Kapuskasing"?

You kidding? You watch the Olympics? They stuffed thirty-six thousand paying customers inside a stadium to watch synchronized swimming! They had people begging scalpers for tickets to watch a guy in a red coat back up his horse! And we have here in our own backyard, hanging off the trees, wild, ravening kamikaze beasts that know no fear, attack like Stuka bombers and thirst for human blood.

Oh no, mosquitos properly merchandized will bring in the sports crowd all right. As for the movie fans—we've got a natural! What we have here is a product that combines the ruthlessness of the great white shark; the M.O. of Dracula; the scope of Hitchcock's *The Birds*; and the gut-quaking naked terror of a Parliament Hill press conference. Oh no, we'll get the movie crowd.

"AND HEAH," as Howard might say, "IS THE KICKAH."
Howard!

Cossell! We can get him! For colour commentary! Sure! He's finished with "Monday Night Football"! Says he's fed up with the crowded arenas, the constant travel and the jocks who infrequently manage to wrestle the mike away from him.

Well Howard, you bring your microphone up here some evening next spring. Long about kickoff time we'll stand you on the shores of a Canadian marsh. No crowds . . . no jocks . . . just a few sprinkles of dried blood on your toupee. We'll show you all the "SHEER, UNMITIGATED TERRORIZATION AND STUPEFYING FRONTAL ASSAULTS THAT YOU CAN GET YOUR MOUTH AROUND."

Let's face it, Howard, for a jaded North American sports audience, it's the least you could do.

THE ETERNAL
WRISTWATCH
WRANGLE

THERE'S MORE TO A CANADIAN spring than blooming crocuses and prodigal robins. There is, for instance, the eternal wristwatch wrangle.

Quick now ... come Sunday, are you going to set your watch ahead an hour or back an hour? I always get it mixed up—providing I remember it at all. Thing that worries me is there's a move afoot to make time-telling even more confusing. The U.S. House of Representatives wants to add four more weeks of Daylight Saving Time to the American calendar. If it goes through, it'll mean a phone call from the Oval Office to Ottawa. Mr. Reagan will tell Mr. Mulroney to leave the big hand right where it is but to move the little hand ahead (or back) one hour. Mr. Mulroney will call a press conference and we'll all have yet another time scheme to befuddle us.

That's not the worst of it. Toronto city council is looking at a scheme that would give us not one, not two but *three* different times—Standard, Daylight Saving and Double Daylight Saving. That would mean changing our watches six times a year. Probably nine and three quarters times in Newfoundland. When you think about it, there's a fair dose of human conceit here. I don't think even the U.S. House of Representatives has the power to change time. Time doesn't change—Time just *is*.

And the concept of "daylight saving." Daylight isn't like Deutchmarks or Corn Flakes tops. Daylight can't be saved. Daylight just sort of dribbles all over the joint at its own pace—like a government deficit or an Ed Broadbent speech.

56

That's the trouble about tinkering with time. Eventually it messes up your head. There's a U.S. senator who went on record as being opposed to Daylight Time, because he thought it would result in an extra hour of sunlight which would damage the U.S. tobacco crop. A lot of U.S. farmers are against a switch because they say it would mean they'd have to milk cows in the dark, which is no fun. Well, if you've ever milked a cow, you know that after the first three or four pulls, it wouldn't be a whole barrel of laughs if you did it on the David Letterman show. As for the cow, well, it's not the hands on any *clock* that she's concerned with. . .

Try to remember this: Spring Ahead, Fall Back. If you're still in trouble—relax. You don't really have to remember anything. There's no law that says you *have* to change your clocks or watches. It's a request. If you want, you can set your Timex to Atlantic, Pacific, Eastern, Central, Rocky Mountain or any other time you feel like. Personally, I'm setting mine to Newfoundland Time. Any zone in which the bad news invariably occurs a half an hour later is a lesson in civility to us all.

A MOOSE ON A HUNGER STRIKE

ANGUS ISN'T SPEAKING TO ME AGAIN. It's an annual trauma. Happens every spring. Angus is a sheep dog.

Usually. Every April or May he undergoes an overnight transformation.

He gets about eighteen pounds of fur clipped off.

The effect is ... amazing. One day you have this shambling mound of fur shuffling around the house, blocking doorways, filling whole chesterfields at a time. The next day it's a skinny little greyhound-y mutt shivering and skulking around like a rat in a rainstorm.

I always feel badly after the shearing. People who've known Angus for years look at the nude version and invariably ask: "What's that?" The German shepherd across the road laughs at him. The dachshund down the street gets lippy. Cats smirk. Angus understands it all. And blames me.

Well it can't be helped. I remember the year I weakened. One spring—there must have been a strong headwind—those big brown pleading eyes got to me. I decided not to have him clipped. That afternoon I took Angus for a walk down in the ravine.

It took three strong men with ropes and a front-end loader to bring him home. Angus had found a burr patch. The next day he got clipped.

Actually, I think Angus would probably welcome the change if they just took off his excess fur and left him looking more or less like a sheep dog. But there's something about Angus that brings out the frustrated architect in human dog clippers.

They regard him as a challenge to their creativity. They shave most of his body down to the skin, but they leave a little Theda Bara fringe of hair across his eyes. They sculpt his ears. They shave most of his tail, but not all of it. They leave a little perky pom-pom fur ball right on the end.

Next to your average city council meeting, there is nothing more ridiculous than a sheep dog masquerading as a poodle.

At least I always thought he looked like a poodle. Last night after the sun was safely down and Angus was willing to take a chance on being seen in public, I took him for a walk down the back lane. Unfortunately, the neighbour was out watering her lawn. She asked the inevitable question.

"What's that?"

"Angus," I answered as he cringed against my leg.

The neighbour sized him up for a moment than turned to water her marigolds.

"Looks like a moose on a hunger strike," she said.

Angus wasn't amused.

WE'RE GOOD ANTS, WE CANADIANS

I IMAGINE AUTUMN IS A lot easier for bears. Bears just eat like pigs, fall into a catatonic snooze and sleep right through the whole frosty final act of the drama. Not just bears either. Autumn is a piece of cake for a lot of Canadian fauna. Frogs dive into the mud, Clydesdales mosey down to the barn for free room and board ... everything with wings, from mallards to monarch butterflies, flaps off to its winter condo, somewhere well south of the Mason-Dixon line.

We two-legged, furless and gravity-bound Canucks don't get off so lightly. We have Things To Fill this time of year. Things like mason jars, fruit baskets, root cellars, freezers, woodboxes, coal bins, oil tanks, car radiators ... and the chequing account to pay for all of the above.

Some Canadians get all a-quiver and dewey-eyed about this time of year. Poets and Vancouverites mostly. For the rest of us, autumn is not all that sublime. For us it's a kind of desperate no-man's land, separating the tyranny we've survived from the one that's about to club us over the head. Winter's coming. That big ugly step-sister of a season that busts out of the attic once a year and makes being Canadian the poignant and soul-strengthening experience that it is.

Autumn is the season about which the "Ant and the Grasshopper" fable was written. You know the one ... decent, hardworking Ant toils diligently by the sweat of his antenna all autumn and lays in supplies for the winter, while decadent, airhead

Grasshopper just parties day and night. A Canadian should have written that fable—maybe between putting down preserves and caulking cracks around the windowframes. We're good ants, we Canadians.

Although I must confess every once in a while I get an urge to chuck the whole thing and find myself a wild all-night grasshopper party . . . or maybe just a bear cave with a room to let.

CHIC IN
THE WINTER

THE BEST THING I KNOW about this winter, so far, is that nobody has come up to me for a good month or so with that standard Canadian, winter opening gambit, "Cold enough for ya?" That particular conversational cliché succumbed to hypothermia back about December 13th, as I recall. The temperature here in Thunder Bay was a piffling 15° or 20° below; but there was a skin-searing howler of a northerly booting it around so that the wind-chill factor made for a temperature of 49° below. Fahrenheit? Celcius? At 49° below on anybody's scale, any living flesh that protrudes from your parka will achieve the consistency of Woolworth china and snap off in about sixty seconds.

Speaking of parkas, I got one for Christmas. It's calf-length and it's down-filled. I figure there are about 1,750 naked mallards shivering on a pond somewhere because of my parka. And if I said I felt guilty about that, I'd be a hypocrite. I'm warm; and I'm glad I'm warm, and I hardly ever think about the nude ducks or the fact that I look like a quilted mummy when I trudge out the door in the morning.

It's a funny country, Canada, especially in the winter. Canucks who live in semi-temperate portions of it like Vancouver, Victoria, Point Pelee or Hamilton, probably don't realize it, but an entire sartorial metamorphosis goes on for all the citizens who live upstairs. During the summer, it's hard to tell a Northerner from a Southerner. We go in for shorts and tank-tops and polyesters and cottons just like you southern natives. But in the winter? Haw! No more foolin' around. Businessmen down there can get by with those nifty, little toe rubbers and three-quarter length, light-weight car coats. We know. Sometimes they visit us here in the winter. We pick them up off the tarmac after they fly in.

Up here, it's parkas, bush boots, moose-hide mitts, scarves, and balaclavas. And we become a community of strangers: bulky, bundled-up wraiths shuffling through the billowing clouds of exhaust, veiled by the sun which staggers into the sky three hours late and retires before the five o'clock whistle blows.

"Whozzat across the street . . . Fred?"

"I dunno; Fred gotta green parka?"

We really ought to wear big numbers on the back, like football players. It's not that way down south, of course. In Montreal, Toronto, Windsor, Victoria, folks there are still into style. We can't do that, those of us who live in Canada's attic. For Southerners, the risk is head colds, blotchy skin—pneumonia . . . tops. Up here, trying for trendy in winter means a brief interlude of frost bite, followed by a blissful feeling of warmth, and then a desire to curl up and go to sleep. We find a few of those each spring when the snowbanks melt.

There's a lot of talk about the "dividedness" of Canada—two solitudes, Ottawa versus the provinces, rural versus urban, nationalists against the separatists, east versus west. I think the really important dividing line is a kind of wavy one that runs from B.C. right to the east coast: the snow belt, maybe, or frost line. It's not really well defined. But if you live below it, you wonder if you should really bother buying snow tires this year. You actually think that three inches of snow is a blizzard: and most important, you worry about how you look when you go out the door on a winter morning. If you live above the line, you don't care if somebody mistakes you for the Goodyear blimp. You fantasize about the day when some enterprising inventor comes up with a down-filled sleeping bag with arms and legs. You think in B.T.U.s. You certainly don't fret about whether your boots match your jacket. You only worry about how much you can put on and still squeeze behind the steering wheel.

We may not be chic in the winter, we Northerners, but we're warm. And if you ever wonder what's going on underneath all

63

those layers of parkas, and bush boots, balaclavas, and elbow-length mitts, well, the truth is, we're thinking about you: chic, stylish, colour-coordinated, southern Canadians, hailing a cab, waiting for your car to warm up, walking the dog. We see you on "The National," you know: standing there, hunched over at the bus stop, shivering in your spiffy little Italian boots. You look good! Blue is definitely your colour. We think about you a lot: and sometimes, in the depths of our snorkle-hooded parkas, we snicker a little.

MORE RESPECT FOR THE BIRDS

Where do the birds sleep?
In the trees.
But how do they sleep?
upright on branches,
leaning against the trunks.
How do they keep from falling?
they sleep and the wind
cradles them.

A FEW LINES FROM A poem by Brenda Fleet. I liked them because I'd never stopped to think about how birds sleep, with their skinny little talons clamped on to a poplar branch or a hydro line. Know what would happen to you or me if we tried to sleep like that? Look Ma—freeform pizza!

That's the thing about birds though ... one doesn't tend to think about them overmuch. Sometimes we borrow their imagined qualities and apply them derisively to fellow humans. As in "turkey," "feather-brain" and "chicken-bleep," not to mention "pigeon-toed" and "crow-footed." I think we are prone to dismiss birds as timid, largely irrelevant and ... well, bird-brained, I guess.

Which is a pity. Birds deserve better than that. Especially in the Respect Department. I remember the very first time it occurred to me that perhaps I should take geese more seriously. I was crossing a barnyard at the time, laden down with two buckets of bran for the horses. Suddenly, bearing down on me like a large white Lancaster bomber, screeching imprecations against me, my family and all my heirs and assigns was—a goose.

I had seen this goose before, waddling about the barnyard. I paid him no more mind than I would a chicken or a turkey or any other feathered farmyard habitué. This was the first time, however, I had placed myself between the goose and a gaggle of goslings he obviously felt rather protective towards. I've been chased by terriers, pomeranians, collies, German shepherds and even one Great Dane, but none of them frightened me more than that goose did.

Which is why a lot of businessmen have decided that the goose makes a better watchdog than watchdogs do. I know of several golf courses, two breweries and even a German munitions factory that have forsaken the services of nightwatchmen and trained dobermans. Now, each evening they just turn a couple of flocks of geese loose on the premises. Any intruder unwise enough to trespass, invariably sets off a cacophony of honking and hissing and flapping and pecking that makes a conventional alarm system sound like a Bing Crosby lullaby.

Speaking of munitions factories, there's one down in Springfield, Massachusetts that's encountered an unusual avian precipitation problem.

At Smith & Wesson headquarters, it's raining golf balls. Smith & Wesson is the largest manufacturer of firearms in the U.S.A. but they don't have the firepower to withstand this invasion. Company executives have been forced to practise broken field running between the parking lot and the office doors as they dodge golf balls falling out of the heavens and boinging off the pavement, windshields and occasionally, well-tonsured executive skulls.

The culprits? Seagulls. The birds have been picking up errant golf balls from the Smith & Wesson Company driving range, taking them up to about five hundred feet and dropping them all around the Smith & Wesson headquarters.

A company spokesman says the seagulls are mistaking golf balls for clams, and dropping them on the ground to smash them open—something that seagulls have been known to do.

With clams.

Personally, I figure the dumbest seagull ever to preen a tail feather could tell the difference between a clam shell and a Spalding Three Dot. I think the gulls are making a political statement about gun control.

On behalf, no doubt, of their defenceless migrating brothers: ducks and geese.

66

FLOGGING THE FLOTSAM AND JETSAM

WHEN YOU FINALLY MAKE your decision to move out of the North, there are a number of gut-wrenching moments and situations to contend with. Tearful goodbyes to old friends ... the mournful cries of a loon at daybreak ... that first glance at the mover's estimate...

But there is another, far more harrowing gauntlet to be run before the North will let you go.

The pre-move yard sale.

We had ours last weekend. The doctors claim I'll be off in-travenous in a couple of days and as long as I keep taking the little purple pills, the nightmares shouldn't come back.

On the off-chance that you ever become foolish enough to contemplate holding a yard sale, let me tell you what I've learned. First off: beware of the "strangers from Calgary." They show up at your front door at dawn on Tuesday morning, unsmiling deadly looking folks with cobra eyes. They want to know if they can have a "sneak preview." Clutching your pajama drawstring defensively, you tell them that the sale doesn't start until Saturday morning. That's when they tell you they're from Calgary and won't be around on Saturday.

They're not from Calgary of course. They are dealers, professional and otherwise, trying to get the jump on the competition and cream off any bargains you might have. Black's advice on how to deal with the Calgary Early Bird sharpies?

Without mercy. Anyone who is loutish enough to wake you up three days before a sale and then lie to you about it, doesn't deserve consideration. Slam the door on 'em. If that doesn't work, phone up your neighbour and ask him to send his dobermans over to play in your front yard.

Another thing you can prepare yourself for in advance is the stark realization of the awesome amount of junk you've accumulated over the years. They're called yard sales, but they should be called arena sales or football field sales, because that's the amount of space you need to accommodate the flotsam and jetsam that you'll be trying to flog.

And *such* flotsam and jetsam! Even after you've weeded out the truly awful crap you'll still have huge mounds and rubbish heaps of effluvia worthy of a fair-sized Appalachian town.

Yard sales give you the opportunity to reassess your position in the cosmos. As reflected in questions such as: "If I'm so smart, how come I've been paying rent on stuff like this for years?"

Oh, yes indeedy. The yard sale is nothing if not a crash course in humility. After all, it's pretty hard to feel proud when a little old lady is holding up a pair of your long johns in the middle of the crowd, asking for a discount because "there's two buttons missing on the trapdoor!"

Which brings us to Black's Piece of Advice Number Two on how to survive your yard sale: Don't Be Proud.

About anything. Remember, the object of this exercise in public flagellation is not to impress your neighbours or outwit the customers or even to make a huge pile of money. The object of the yard sale is to *unload the junk*.

And you will. As long as you don't get proud ("Give me back those Stanfields lady ... you don't deserve to buy them!") Or greedy. Just because you paid $11.95 for your hardcover copy of *Sociological Imperatives Among the Watusi* doesn't mean you'll get anything like that at your sale.

Other morsels of advice? Well, make sure you've got lots of change—in coins and bills. I still have fond memories of the lady who paid for two used comic books with a fifty-dollar bill. Get lots of signs up around the neighbourhood—particularly around busy intersections—and for crying out loud make them big enough to read from a passing car.

One final tip—well, I guess this is more of a request actually—do you think you could give me a phone call, here at the paper, two or three days before you advertise the sale?

It's not for me, you understand. It's just that I have these two friends from Calgary staying with me...

68

WHACKY ANIMALS

MAYBE IT'S BECAUSE I WAS starved for animal companionship as a child. Perhaps it's a direct result of having watched Hitchcock's *The Birds* on late night TV too many times. Or it could be that I'm just a pervert, I guess. All I know for sure is: I love those "whacky animal" news stories. I've got three of 'em for you today.

The first story concerns one of the whackiest animals of all time: Mister Godzilla. Remember Godzilla? He was a colossal, arthritic, mutant lizard that terrorized the citizenry of Tokyo in sixteen different and uniformly terrible movies back in the fifties. Godzilla swatted down condos with his tail and played crack-the-whip with commuter trains, all while routinely fricaseeing Japanese Air Force jet fighters with one huff of his molten lizard breath.

I thought it was all over for the big lug when he disappeared beneath the scum of Tokyo Harbour at the end of Son-Of-Godzilla's - Second - Nephew - By - Marriage - Meets - Ma - And - Pa - Kettle-In-Disneyworld—or whatever that last Godzilla movie was called.

But no. The word is that an all-new Godzilla flick is poised to lumber onto a movie screen near you—perhaps as early as this spring. Which just goes to show that you can't keep a good lizard down.

Also hot off the grapevine: The Boozing Bruin of Nova Scotia. Seems there's been a bit of vandalism around some of the summer

69

camps in Guysborough County, N.S. Five different camps have been broken into, and in each case, valuables such as radios, binoculars and rifles were untouched. All that's missing is the booze. All that's been added are bear tracks. One investigator reported: "At one camp, the bear bit off the neck of a 40-ouncer, downed the contents, and placed the empty back on the table, as if he wanted a refill." The same bear also found a liquor cache outside the camp. He dug that up and drank it dry, too.

Authorities are trying to live trap the interloper, fast. Preferably while he's sleeping off this bender. They know exactly what to look for. A black bear.

With a red nose.

One last story before we slam the cage door. This one comes out of Switzerland, where a group of doctors report that they've had to treat more than a dozen joggers over the past two years, all suffering from the same, ah . . . ailment. Buzzard attacks.

Yep. The runners complain that European Buzzards—and even some other birds of prey—have been divebombing them. The doctors' report indicates the birds repeatedly swoop down on the plodding bipeds (usually from behind) leaving scratched scalps and pecked pates in their wake.

The joggers say that this is no—you will pardon the pun—lark. The birds are vicious. They also report that the attacks cease the moment the victims stop jogging.

Well, I dunno.

I've never been a major booster of jogging (or any other form of self-flagellation) but to paraphrase Voltaire, I am willing to defend to the death your right to indulge.

That's *your* death, of course.

I submit that when you engage in an activity vile enough to offend buzzards, it is time to re-examine your recreational alternatives.

PREDICTING THE
UNPREDICTABLE

I'M NOT SURE WHEN I stopped listening to weather forecasts on the radio. I know that something snapped one day last
winter when I heard the weatherman telling me the wind chill
factor in watts per square metre. But I think my attention was
drifting before that. You see, as a non-sailing, non-farming, non-
bush-plane-piloting member of the urban proletariat, my weather
needs are fairly few. I've never been able to make much use of the
relative humidity index or barometric fluctuations up and down or
wind direction and speed. Weather forecasts, where I live, tell me
all those things ... and more ... and not just for the street where
I live or the office where I work. They tell me about Arctic highs
and Prairie troughs, about midwestern droughts and East Coast
gales. Interesting ... but not what I need when I'm trying to
figure out what length underwear to put on in the morning.

Well, I bring glad tidings. It says in my newspaper that Alan
Cambell, head of public and marine weather services for Environment Canada, has launched a study to find out what Canadians
really want in their weather forecasts. Why? Because, says Alan
Cambell, they've noticed a few flaws in the forecasts we get now.

"Most Canadian city dwellers," opines this wonderful man, who
has my vote for prime minister if he wants it, "want only two
pieces of information: whether it's going to rain or snow ... and
what the temperature is going to be."

Right *on*, Mr. Cambell!

He says that some of the forecast data we get is redundant. "If it's going to rain," he says, "there's very little point in saying that it's going to be cloudy."

Right again, Mr. Cambell!

Even though some radio forecasts are "long-winded" (Mr. Cambell's words, not mine)—he points out that they still don't tell us some things we really could stand to know. Things like . . . "Today will be *warmer* than yesterday." Or, "You might want to throw a sweater in the back seat for later this afternoon when the wind picks up."

Wouldn't it be lovely to hear *that* on the Environment Canada forecasts? Instead of things like: "Possibility of precipitation 10 percent today, 10 percent tonight, 10 percent tomorrow." What does that mean anyway? That it's going to rain on 10 percent of the forecast area? Or that 10 percent of my picnic stands a 10 percent chance of getting damp?

Speaking of "what does it mean?" what does "partly cloudy" mean? As opposed to "partly sunny" I mean? Is "cloudy" the same as "overcast"? Are "mainly clear" skies anything like "mostly sunny skies"? And "variable cloudiness" . . . what exactly is that? My dictionary says "variable" means changeable. Changeable clouds? Into what? Are we talking transvestism here? The Three Faces of Eve? Water into Wine? The Philosopher's Stone?

Don't mistake me. I'm not making mock of the wallahs who toil for Environment Canada. They are intelligent, hardworking, underpersonned and faced with an impossible task: predicting the unpredictable. I'm just glad that they've decided to take a crack at comprehensibility.

More power to you, Alan Cambell, head of public and marine weather services for Environment Canada. Let your forecasts be right or wrong or half of each—but clear! And short!

Let's leave the excessive cloud cover and gusty, blustery winds where they belong. In the House of Commons.

QUEEN VICTORIA, A FINE CHARACTER

WELL I SEE MAY 24th falls on May the 20th this year. Victoria Day, I mean. One of our more confusing national holidays. Which is apt—because there's a fair bit of confusion surrounding the lady the day is named after.

Victoria was tiny, kind of dumpy and exceedingly green when she took over management of the world's largest firm at the age of eighteen. She held the job for the next sixty-four years. When she died in 1901 her name was on an Australian state, a Canadian provincial capital, the third largest lake in the world, a huge African waterfall, several mountains, half a dozen rivers, a giant island in the Arctic, a huge chunk of Antarctica, a medal for bravery, a touring car, God nows how many ships, a Canadian holiday and ... an age. An age which all right-thinking modern folk snicker at. The Victorian Age. Synonymous with pomposity. Hypocrisy. Repression. Stuffiness. Inhibition.

Inhibited? Victoria proposed to Prince Albert because she thought he'd never work up the nerve. Repressed? Listen to this quote: "So excessively handsome, such beautiful blue eyes, an exquisite nose and such a pretty mouth ... a beautiful figure, broad in the shoulders and a fine waist." That's Queen Vicky describing her husband. She had a taste for Mariani wine, which is a sipping by-product of the same substance that got Richard Pryor and John De Lorean in trouble.

She flirted with Disraeli, and there's some evidence she took a servant as a lover after Albert died. Perhaps even bore him a son.

This is a woman who gave Mount Kilimanjaro to a nephew as a birthday present; who picked Ottawa as the capital of our country on the basis of a Gatineau Hills watercolour she had fancied.

Near as I can figure, Queen Victoria was about as Victorian as Eartha Kitt. You know who was Victorian? Prince Albert, that's who. Albert once described his wife as: "a fine character but warped in many respects by wrong upbringing."

The Duke of Wellington, who was not exactly Tom Cruise himself, observed: "Prince Albert was extremely straightlaced and rather a stickler for morality, while she ... was rather the other way."

My kind of people. Think about Victoria—the real Victoria—this Victoria Day. And do something uncharacteristic for Canadians. Enjoy yourself.

Unless of course you happen to live in Prince Albert.

VACATION ONE-UPMANSHIP

WELL, WHAT WITH THE LEAFS AND THE Ti Cats both out on the golf greens, it makes for long pauses in the cocktail chatter circuit. Luckily, a brand new game has swum in to fill the vacuum. It's called ... I dunno what it's called. Call it Vacation One-upmanship, I guess. Way it works, is somebody sidles up to you at the chip dip to ask about your tan. You tell them you spent ten days at Myrtle Beach. They smile faintly and announce that they wintered on a yacht in the Aegean, reconstructing Ancient Greek amphitheatres on the weekends. You counter with the fact that two years ago you did a tour of the Yucatan by llama caravan. They come back with a tale of nude kayaking in the Himalayas.

The point of the game is to "out-exotic" your opponent ... but I think Canadians have earned a "Bye" in this contest. Anywhere in the world is better than Canada in January. Any port in a storm —in fact any *storm* in a storm—as long as it doesn't feature ice pellets, snowdrifts or a windchill factor. When the object is fleeing a Canadian winter, you just can't *flunk* vacations.

But that's winter. *This* time of year is quite a different story. Come the spring thaw, and Canada becomes not a half bad place to plant your beach umbrella. Look at the advantages. The natives are friendly, the water's good, you can trust the food and speak the language. You even know the currency—well, as well as Michael Wilson does, anyway.

Oh sure, it has its downside—mosquitoes, the odd heat wave

... but would you trade your calamine lotion for, say, dysentery in Cuernavaca? Care to swap an overheated rad on the Trans-Canada for an all-night vigil in the Lost Luggage Temple at Bangkok International, fending off cockroaches the size of sports cars while you wait for your Samsonite to show? Of course not.

You know if you really want to win at Vacation One-upmanship, the trick is to let your opponent score early with hot air ballooning over Brazilia or snorkeling in Lake Titticaca ... then you yawn discreetly and allow as how you very seldom bother leaving Canada for vacations anymore—what with the superb white water rafting in Yukon Territory; the luxury liner trips through the Northwest Passage ... and the thrill of baitcasting for trophy cod from a Grand Banks dory.

But wherever you go, at home or abroad, you can always use a few travel tips. Here are a couple from a seasoned road veteran who's been as far afield as Steinbach and all the way down to North Tonawanda, New York. One: When hitchhiking, try to look like the people you hope will pick you up. Two: Always pack twice as much money and half as many clothes as you think you'll need. And three: if you return home looking anything like your passport photo—take a couple of weeks off just to poke around the house. You need a rest.

A NECKLACE OF NUGGETS

AH ME, IT MUST BE SPRING. I find it impossible to hold a thought for more than a few seconds. I think I sat down just now to write a column, but I can't remember the topic. What I'll give you instead is a crude little necklace of nuggets panned from the raging grey torrent of newsprint that smudges these fingers each week. Small stories in the news that didn't quite make the headlines.

The first item comes from the Middle East—about seven miles outside of Jerusalem. A good working title might be: What Hath Walt Wrought?

Walt Disney, I'm referring to. We're all familiar with Disneyworld and Disneyland. Did anyone doubt that Bibleland could be far behind? Yes, Bibleland. It's a hundred-million-dollar tourist attraction and it's underway right now. When it opens its polyurethaned St. Peter's Gates, visitors who've bought tickets will be able to command the Red Sea (a scale model, natch) to part. They'll have an opportunity to purchase a whole series of souvenirs based on tales from both the Old and the New Testament—and on the drawing board right now, what promises to be a real crowd-pleaser: autographed copies of the Ten Commandments, sold by a tall guy in a big, bushy beard.

You'll know him right away. He'll have a button on his robe that'll read, "Hi! I'm Moses!"

. . .

From our The-Times-They-Ain't-A-Changin'-As-Fast-As-We-

77

Thought Department, news of a brand new cookbook, from a somewhat unexpected cookbook author. The book is called *Barbecuing With Bobby* and it's written by ... Bobby Seale.

Yep. The old Black Panther hisself. An ex-member of The Chicago Seven, Bobby's traded in his leather jacket and black beret for ... well, for an apron that reads "Come n' Get It!" Kinda puts a whole new slant on the Panther slogan "Burn, Baby, burn" doesn't it?

Ah, but I can sense all you Born-Again-Woodstockian, Harrowsmithite, Seize-The-Time-Blowing-In-the-Winders getting depressed out there. We can't have that. This is the eighties, right? Where good news is the only news we wanna hear.

Awright awready. Here's a Happy Face news story about one of the most miserable institutions of modern time: Income Tax. It seems that down in the U.S., the Internal Revenue Service has had a change of heart and decided to lighten up on a tax transgressor.

The criminal party in the case is the Rohm and Haas Company —one of the largest chemical manufacturers in North America. The company was facing a late payment penalty from the IRS to the tune of $47,000. It wasn't that Rohm and Haas had tried to avoid paying its taxes. Oh no. The company had sent in a cheque for more than four million bucks. $4,488,112.88 to be precise. But that was the problem. According to the IRS ferrets, Rohm and Haas really owed $4,488,112 and ... *ninety*-eight cents.

Rohm and Haas was a dime short.

Accordingly, the IRS slapped Rohm and Haas with a $47,000 fine. Well, it only took five company lawyers and a half a year of legal wrangling, but finally the Internal Revenue Service dropped the late penalty payment against Rohm and Haas. The IRS didn't apologize of course. No sense in being downright wimpy.

Makes you want to think twice before you open your Revenue Canada refund envelope, doesn't it?

PART 3
STILL PUDGY AFTER ALL THESE YEARS

STILL PUDGY AFTER ALL THESE YEARS

I DON'T KNOW ABOUT YOU, but I'm fed up with the whole concept. Thinness, I mean. I've tried 5BX. I've tried the Hollywood Diet. I've done Drinking Man's, Scarsdale, the Hilton, the Hollywood, the Dachman Permanent Weight Loss, Dr. Cooper's Fabulous Fructose, the Beverley Hills, the Loma Linda Vegetarian, the Pritikin, the (Argh!) Sexibody, the Liquid Protein, the Southhampton, the Berkowitz, the Atkins, the Starch Blockers, the Richard Simmons. . .

And I'm fat.

Just about the way I was—give or take a kilopascal—before I started reading up on diets a hundred thousand light years ago. Wotta drag! I've eschewed at one time or another: carbohydrates, protein, polyunsaturates, alcohol, fried foods, starches, meat products, dairy foods and things containing the letter *R*.

And I'm still fat.

Not that I've just fooled around with my diet. Oh no. I've altered my lifestyle too. I gave up smoking. I joined the "Y." I quit carousing and hanging around with the low-life riff raff I enjoyed and took to hanging around with lean people with thin lips and positive outlooks on life. There was a period in my life when my idea of a fabulous time was to party flat-out through the night and watch the sun come up over the rim of my marguerita glass. No more. Now I start to yawn when the streetlights come on. I have yet to make it all the way through "The Journal" with my eyes open, and David Letterman is just some curious televised phenomenon that everybody else has seen but me.

Did I mention jogging? Oh yes, I do that too. I hate every lung-searing, leg-aching moment of it, but I jog. And swim. And risk turning myself into someone's free form hood ornament by riding my bike several miles a day.

80

And why? Why do I voluntarily pursue the painful, joyless life of a Dominican monk-cum-health freak? Why, to be thin of course.

Except I'm not. I am, as previously hinted at, still pudgy after all these years.

But you know what really hurts? Not the hours of fruitless perspiration or the gross tonnage of beer, peanuts, gravy and banana splits not ingested, no. What hurts is discovering, at this late stage of the Avoirdupois Wars, the existence of Henllys Hall.

Henllys Hall is a fifty-acre resort on the island of Anglesey, off the coast of Wales.

Actually, it's not a resort. It's a fat farm.

Hold on now! I don't mean an American-style fat farm, such as the places Elizabeth Taylor goes every six months or so to shed half a hundredweight. I mean a *Fat Farm*. A place where fat people go to . . . get *fatter*!

Yes! At Henllys Hall, the first-time visitor is greeted with a personal tray of gloppy, gooey, calorie-saturated cakes and pastries. When he gets to his room the visitor finds mounds of handmade chocolates, chips and peanuts on the nighttable. And the meals? Steaks, smothered in gravy, tons of cream sauces, puddings, pies, french fries with everything. Breakfast is a modest orgy of fried eggs, bacon, sausages, with fried bread and potatoes —all you can eat. But not before ten in the morning, please.

Mind you it's not all over-indulgence at Henllys Hall—one has to have rules, after all. Accordingly, there is a strict ban on granola, muesli, lettuce leaves, raw carrots—anything remotely health-promoting. Sneakers and exercise gear are similarly prohibited—in fact all exercise above and beyond elbow bending, biting and swallowing is distinctly frowned upon.

Gross? Well yeah, I suppose it is. Fun to fantasize about, though. And you can bet that tomorrow morning, when my swollen trotters are pounding down the road at the end of my morning run, I won't have visions of half a grapefruit and a slice of dry toast dancing before my eyes. Nope, I'll be thinking about a great, greasy breakfast in bed at Henllys Hall.

Mmmmmmmmm. Almost enough to make a guy look forward to jogging.

THE SIEVE MEMORY SYNDROME

AS FAR AS I'M CONCERNED, a writer by the name of Austin O'Malley said all there is to say about memory. "Memory" wrote Mr. O'Malley, "is a crazy woman who hoards coloured rags and throws away food." If we at least got to *vote* on what gets hoarded and what gets thrown out! I, for instance, would cheerfully consign the Pythagorean Theorem, which I remember perfectly, to the dustbin of oblivion in return for being allowed to remember say, my postal code, the name of that great Chinese restaurant or the combination to the lock that's kept my ten speed in chains in the basement for the past six weeks. I can recall exactly how a corner fish and chip shop smelled on Friday afternoons on my way home from public school ... but when I reach for the gas cap on my car, I never remember whether it's clockwise or counter-clockwise to loosen. At least I can't remember until I've reefed it the wrong way and all but welded the cap to my car while giving myself a hernia.

But drawing a blank with inanimate objects isn't so bad. It's forgetting people that I'm really skilled at.

You know the old cliché: "I can't remember names, but I never forget a face"? Well, you'll never hear that line from me. I forget *both*. Or even worse—I *transpose*. Grafting some incongruous moniker onto a totally undeserving recipient. Take Garth, for instance. Every time I run into the owner of the hardware store in town, I say: "How's it goin', Garth?"

His name isn't Garth. The only Garth I ever knew in my life

was a drunk who tried to borrow twenty bucks off me in a bar in Antigua five years ago. My hardware store man doesn't look remotely like the Antiguan barfly. He's not even the right colour. And anyway, his name is Bill. I know that, because he took out his business card, circled the "Bill" and tucked it into my shirt pocket the last time I said: "How's it goin', Garth?"

There are ways to combat the Sieve Memory Syndrome. I read a book about it once. The book promised to teach me how to remember names and faces easily . . . all I had to do was *learn to associate*, it said. Soon as someone's introduced to you, you associate the name with . . . a friend or a movie star . . . or maybe with an occupation. If the stranger's name is Taylor, picture him with a thimble in his mouth. If a lady's name is Singer, visualize her hitting high *C* at the Met. Or, suggested the book, rhyme the stranger's name with something—plain Jane, Fred the Head, Bob the Slob . . . that kind of thing.

Oh, I tell ya, I was feeling pretty cocky at the next cocktail party I went to. Until the host came up with a dark haired, sullen looking woman in tow and said: "Art, so glad you could make it . . . I'd like you to meet a member of the Spanish aristocracy—this is Her Grandeloquencia Senora Maria Theresa Hortensia Francesca de la Renuncia"—or something like that. I must confess I wasn't paying real close attention, preoccupied as I was with trying to remember the name of my host.

What's depressing is that I'm still young! Well, not loaf of bread, jug of wine, NHL-tryout young maybe . . . but a long way from a toothless, doddering, aged, greybeard elder. Pretty young. Which means that despite my inability to recall my office phone number; whether I filed an income tax return last April, or the name of the nice, and I might add very capable, radio producer looking back at me through the glass right now—despite the very demonstrable evidence that I'm thoroughly adrift in the sea of forgetfulness. I still have senility to look forward to.

SIX RULES FOR A
LONG LIFE

The years dwindle down
To a precious few ...

FOR ME, THOSE WERE JUST lines from an old Sinatra ballad until a few years back. I remember the date exactly, as a matter of fact—September, 1984. That's when Sophia Loren and Brigitte Bardot both turned fifty.

Sophia? Fifty? Brigitte? A half-century old? Doesn't seem possible—not that fifty is so awfully old, you understand—I'm within hobbling distance of it myself. But it's okay when people like me turn fifty—that's nothing. It's different for ageless legends like Brigitte and Sophia. I've had a lot of fantasies over the years about those two. Imagining either of them as a grandmother wasn't one of them.

Ironically, Sophia seems to be handling her age a lot more gracefully than I am. Like wine and violins, she just gets better with age. Did you see that big coffee table book by Karsh—a lavish collection of photographs of the world's most glamorous people, taken by Canada's most famous photographer? That was Sophia on the front cover. Forty-nine and more gorgeous than ever.

And *La BB*? She is—*hélas*—not taking it so well. She's shunned the limelight for the past several years and she tends to throw things at people who point cameras at her. Recently in a rare interview she talked about how she felt about her birthday.

"It's really tough to age," mourned Brigitte, "...it's half a century. Welcome to the senior citizens' club."

Mademoiselle Bardot's not just being melodramatic either. On her forty-ninth birthday she tried to do herself in. Shucks, Brigitte ... it's not all that grim. I recall a sex goddess a little before your time who handled the aging process with a little humour. Her name was Gypsy Rose Lee and she was a stripper. When asked how she felt about "becoming mature," Gypsy sniffed, "I have everything I had twenty years ago—except now it's all lower."

I like Satchel Paige's philosophy even better. Mr. Paige was the ageless pitcher who hurled in the Negro Baseball League way back in the twenties. And thirties. And forties. As a matter of fact, Satchel Paige pitched three scoreless innings for the Kansas City Athletics in 1965.

Naturally, a lot of people were curious about Satchel and how he stayed so young. They got so curious that Satch got a card printed up which he would hand out. The card was entitled "Satchel Paige's Six Rules For a Long Life."

- Don't eat fried meats. They angry up the blood.
- If your stomach disputes you, lie down and pacify it with cool thoughts.
- Keep the juices flowing by jangling gently when you walk.
- Go very light on vices. The social ramble ain't restful.
- Avoid running at all times.
- Don't look back. Something might be gaining on you.

The one thing that Ol' Satch would not give out was his true age. As he explained to one particularly persistent reporter after a game, "Look. How old would you be if you didn't know how old you was?"

WHAT IS THIS THING CALLED LOVE

THERE ARE MANY curious and contrary conditions on the
battered face of this planet, but one of the most curious and
contrary (some would go as far as ornery) conditions is this thing
called love. As in "What is this thing called Love?"

That's a poser that's been batted around by poets and politicians and plebs on the street for many thousands of years, probably
since the first shaggy caveman looked up from his raw, half-eaten
pterodactyl haunch into the eyes of his greasy, grunting companion, and felt what American screenwriter Ben Hecht poignantly
described as "something like a hole in the heart."

Lotta writers have taken a run at definitions of love. Many of
them were gaga and gooey and obviously afflicted with the disease
they were trying to describe. I prefer the bitter-sweet definitions
—the assessments of observers who have been through the mill
and come to their conclusions downstream.

Maurice Chevalier once said: "Many a man has fallen in love
with a woman in light so dim he would not have chosen a suit by
it."

Zsa Zsa Gabor said: "People in love are incomplete until they
are married; then they are finished." Somerset Maugham described love as: "the dirty trick Nature plays on us to achieve
continuation of the species."

Herewith, three late-twentieth century love stories—all culled
from recent editions of the dailies—all proving that love, if not
blind, could certainly use corrective lenses.

Story the first: from Houston. About a man trying to be Sir Lancelot, and turning out more like Sancho Panza. Our hero was driving through the country one evening when he spotted a partially clad, young woman who appeared to be struggling with a man in the underbrush. He slammed on the brakes; the couple scrambled into a car and drove away. Our hero followed, saw the couple go into a house. He paused only to phone the police, then scrambled over the hedge and sneaked in across the back yard. He was kicking in the back door just as police were storming through the front door, guns drawn. Would have been a heroic story if the man and woman hadn't been ... man and wife ... with a passion for outdoor passion. The rescuer wanted to charge the husband with rape; the husband wanted to charge the rescuer with break and entry. The woman? We're not sure what she wanted. She was last seen slapping the hero's face and flouncing out the front door, clad in a bath towel, shouting at her husband that she would kill him if he ever got her involved in that sort of thing again.

A Canadian love story next. It involves two Torontonians—both financial analysts—who are divorcing one another. They're into a huge custody wrangle that's going all the way to the Ontario Supreme Court. Two youngsters involved, three-and-a-half-year-old brothers. At the moment the separated adults share custody of the minors on a month-by-month basis. The wife has them right now, next month they go to live with the husband. They're both going for total custody. The wife's affidavit reads: "I have become extremely attached to them. I consider them an essential element of my emotional well-being and they are irreplaceable to me."

The husband's affidavit is similarly strong. It says: "I was and am deeply attached to these two. They have been personified to the point where they are more like my children than my pets."

Oh, right. I forgot to mention that the two three-and-a-half-old brothers being fought over are not kids ... but cats.

One last story on the eternal loopiness of love, and then I'll stop. Honest. This one is about an apartment fire in Winnipeg. No injuries—well, maybe a little singed pride. The fire was caused by a wife who grew furious as she waited for her husband to come home one night. And waited, and waited... Finally she blew her top and started the fire. Police have charged her with "setting fire to a substance." The substance? Her husband's baseball cap. She set it in an ashtray and torched it. Was feeling quite good too, until the drapes caught. Twenty-five thousand dollars damage.

Love. Think of all the songsters who have written about it. All the writers from Chaucer to Cheevers; from Plato to McKuen...

One of my favourite observations goes like this: "Love is a wonderful thing, but as long as it's blind, I will never be out of a job." That could have been written by a poet or a philosopher or a songwriter. But it wasn't. It was written by one Justice Selby, U.S. Divorce Court Judge.

TO EVERY MAN THERE IS A SEASON

YOU MAY NOT REALIZE it, but you're reading the words of a common house sparrow. An ex-house sparrow actually. Bland and nondescript? Not me. Not since I discovered that I'm a winter. Winters are big on vivid colours. Fire engine red, lemon yellow ... hot turquoise. Not like your summers. Summers are pastels. Springs and autumns, they're something else again. Springs are the warm, clear shades ... while autumns look best in rich, earth colours. Or maybe it's the other way around. Doesn't matter. It's all here ... in this book, *Colours For Men*. This book reveals that to every man there is a season, and each season has a whole palette of colours. A man who knows how to use his colours can transform himself from a house sparrow to a tail-twitching peacock overnight.

How do you figure out which season you belong to? Well, it's complex. Has to be, otherwise who'd lay out twenty-seven bucks for the book? But basically, any given guy's season depends on his skin tone and eye colour and shade of hair and his "colour history," what colours have worked for him in the past. But trust the book! All God's chillun got seasons, and once you've found yours, turned the keys to your clothes closet over to the Salvation Army, and dropped a couple of thou into an all new wardrobe, then the world is your colour-coordinated oyster. You will look— the book practically guarantees it—younger, healthier, hand-somer, more vital and more confident. Your skin will glow. Lines and wrinkles will simply melt away.

And we are talking all sectors of your till-this-moment-ineffec-tual-and-meaningless life, you understand. Each season features heavy-duty-getting-down-to-business colours; low-key-power-be-hind-the-throne colours ... not to mention gypsy-violins-candle-light-and-chianti, your-place-or-mine colours too.

Just follow your tone chart and you too can metamorphose from a pasty-faced wimp into a take-charge Conrad Black/ Casanova combo ... with just a pinch of Mitchell Sharp tossed in for leavening.

You'll stand out! When you're in a restaurant and some three-hundred-pound dowager goes down choking on a fishbone two tables away, the entire room will instinctively assume that anyone as poised and radiant as you *must* know the Heimlecher Manoeuvre. They'll all stand back, waiting for you to take charge! Yessir, when you're wearing your colours, *all* the less flamboyant bourgeoisie will automatically gravitate toward you, like Junebugs to a glowing McDonalds arch. You'll attract them all ... neurotics, psychotics, hypochondriacs, pedantics, travelling salesmen, born again proselytizers ... joggers...

You know, on second thought ... two things occur to me. One is that the common house sparrow is a lot smarter than he looks ... the second is that when it comes to a coordinating theme for a guy's wardrobe, there's a lot to be said for the old army camou-flage motif.

BRING ON THE KETCHUP

SPEAKING AS A VETERAN of some eight days, two hours and sundry minutes (well ... twenty-nine minutes, but who's counting?)—speaking as a kind of expert, I think it's significant that 75 percent of the word "diet" spells "die."

Halfway through a two-week diet plan, dying doesn't look all that grim. You want grim? I can give you grim. A slice of dry unbuttered protein bread—that's grim. Half a grapefruit with no sugar is grim. Honking and threading your way home through the traffic after a hard day of forelock tugging and back biting at the office—only to face a plate with a glop of cold tuna perforated by a half dozen carrot sticks, with a glass of water chaser—*now*, we're into grim.

Yes, I'm on a diet. The Scarsdale Diet. You remember? Doctor Herman Tarnower's? The man who was shot by a woman? A *thin* woman, significantly enough.

The Scarsdale Diet swept the continent a few years ago and it finally fetched up at my door. This is the famous diet on which you can lose up to (love it—"up to") fourteen pounds in fourteen days and (this is the kicker) never feel hungry.

Well, I feel compelled to report (being as I am, eight days, two hours and—what is it, thirty-one minutes?—into the diet that it's true. You do not feel hungry on this diet. Per se.

You do not feel "hunger." What you do feel are cravings. Obsessive, maniacal cravings for, oh, a cheeseburger with the works. A Labatt's Blue with beads of condensation budding on the label. A mound of golden, glistening french fries. An egg salad sandwich. A swiss mocha Baskin Robbins double decker in a sugar cone . . . a slug of milk right out of the carton. A cold wiener. A fist full of peanut butter.

Heh heh heh.

You can't have any of those things on the Scarsdale Diet. Not even once. I know. I've been on the diet for eight days, two hours and oh must be—yes, my stopwatch says exactly thirty-one minutes now.

(*sigh*) Ahem.

One thing the diet does almost immediately, is to alter your perceptions of food. Take celery sticks. I think it is safe to say that I had journeyed to this point in my alloted earthly span without ever once seriously contemplating the complexities and the finer points of celery sticks—at least up until eight and a bit days ago.

Ever see the movie *An American Werewolf In London*? Remember how the werewolf hit his victims? Like Mean Joe Greene with rabies? Whammo! That's what I do to celery sticks now. Peregrine falcons do not do to pigeons what I do to celery sticks. Slingshot dragsters should move so fast. Atom smashers should have my punch.

Whoo! Eight days, two hours, thirty-one make it thirty-two minutes. Not too bad. Leaves me with only five days, twenty-one hours and twenty-eight—heck might as well call it twenty-seven —minutes to go.

Mind you I'm not going to have a big blowout when I come off the diet in . . . oh yeah. I already covered that. Nope, that's the whole point of the Scarsdale diet—any good diet really. Behaviour modification. All new eating habits. Eat what you need, not what you can stuff in. I mean, as an intelligent rational being with free will, why should there be any problem? There won't be for me in just five short days, twenty-one hours and twenty-six minutes thirty seconds. Or whatever it is. No . . . I'm going to celebrate D-Day with perhaps a small salad . . . a slice of protein bread and one french fry.

No, two. Six. Make it a plate full—small plate. Big plate. And gravy. Lotsa gravy. Yeah and two cinammon coated chocolate dipped double glazed donuts with strawberry centres and a malted milkshake. No two malteds . . . and ketchup. Bring ketchup. Did I forget ketchup? Butter. Whipped cream . . .

COMPUTER LOVE IN THE YEAR 2000

I KNOW I TEND to talk rather overmuch about computer technology. That's because it frightens me. You have to remember that as a creature dog-paddling through the Age of Technology, I am basically comfortable with the pencil sharpener and the bicycle. And I'm talking about manually operated pencil sharpeners and CCM one-speeds. When bikes started sprouting affectations like derailleurs and ten forward gears, they left me behind and befuddled. They became as comprehensible as the control panel in the cockpit of a Concorde jet.

You can appreciate that a man who finds a so-called simple carburetor as full of mystery as say, laser surgery—is going to have trouble with computers.

Turns out I've got more trouble than even I imagined. I learned that last year the Government of Ontario asked the engineering departments of two universities—Carlton and Ottawa—to look into the impact computer technology will have on all us peons between now and the year 2000.

Well the engineering departments have just published their report, and I'm more nervous than ever. The report is full of wonders-of-the-future stuff that we've all grown used to. No more mowing lawns for instance—by the turn of the century robots will take care of that. Snail-like letter delivery will be a thing of the past, says the report. For that matter, letters will be extinct too. Our "mail" will be delivered electronically right to the old TV screen. And in seconds, not days or weeks.

93

The engineers say there will be no more of those excruciating tribal negotiations with garage mechanics: "Whaddya think, Rocco? Every time I turn left and step on the gas it goes tiddlybum tiddlybum. What's that sound like to you?"

No more of that. Your car will have its own built-in computer. The computer will tell you when the car needs fixing and what's wrong with it, to boot.

Well, I can handle all that stuff—I've been reading similar predictions in *Popular Mechanics* since the 1940s.

No, it's something else in this engineering report about technology at the turn of the century that disturbs me. A totally new computer danger that I never thought of. The report says that home computers will be as common in the year 2000 as telephones are right now.

But they're not talking about the dinky little screens with push button controls that we have now. No, they're talking about *talking* computers. How do you program these things? You talk to them. Tell them what you want and when you want it, and they say the equivalent of "Gotcha Chief," and start to hum.

And therein lies the new danger. The engineers say that speech recognition and synthesis will make the new computers almost human. Not only that, emotions will be built into the computer's personality—emotions like sympathy and affection. The authors say there's a very real possibility that by the year 2000, humans could be experiencing "deep emotional involvement" with their home computers.

Well that's just engineer talk—they're really saying there's a good chance people are going to fall in love with their computers.

Well, I should think so. Sympathy ... affection ... understanding ... all from one unit that never looks at other computer owners, doesn't talk back and can fill out your income tax form? I'd be surprised if members of the opposite sex ever look at one another again.

I'd be really terrified by the implications of this engineers report—if I thought there was a chance of these predictions coming true.

I don't. As I said, I've been reading *Popular Mechanics* magazines since the fifties. Remember some of those old magazines?

They used to predict that in the near future, we'd be living in mile-high cities; scooting to work in our personal jet-cars; winging off to space for a weekend on Mars or Venus, all in the near future.

The near future in those magazines was usually seen as the eighties. Well we're here, and it just didn't happen.

I'm no prophet. I don't know what kind of world we'll face in the year 2000. I pray that our biggest problem is a rash of computer love. But I'd be willing to bet one thing. I'll be driving something in the year 2000. It may be a jet-car or a magnetic boat. Or the way it's holding on it may even be my old rattletrap Volvo. But whatever it is, sooner or later I'll find myself talking to some guy in greasy coveralls, and I'll be saying: "Whaddya think Rocco? Every time I turn left and step on the gas it goes tiddlybum tiddlybum. What's that sound like to you?"

And Rocco 2000 will say: "Eet sounds expaaansive."

CANADA'S TRUE NATIONAL SPORT

THIS GAME APPEARS TO BE *a most fascinating one and the men get wildly excited about it. But there can be no doubt as to its roughness, and if the players get over keen and lose their tempers as they are apt to do, the possession of the stick and the close proximity to one another gives the occasion for many a nasty hit. Tonight one man was playing with his nose badly broken and the game had twice to be stopped, once because a man got hit in the mouth and the other time because one of the captains was knocked down unconscious and had to be carried out.*

Well, what the heck—same old Saturday night down at the hockey rink, right? The Soo Greyhounds playing the Sudbury Wolves maybe ... or perhaps the Flyers squaring off against the Islanders. Just an effete European visitor's first-time impressions of a typical game of good old Canadian shinny?

Yes and no. It's a description of a Canadian hockey game all right. It comes from Lady Aberdeen's journal. What's disconcerting is the fact that those two unnamed teams went through their bumps and grinds almost a century ago. The date of the entry reads January 20, 1894.

Imagine that—1894! Canada was only twenty-seven years old and already we were hacking out our international image as hewers of ankles and drawers of hemoglobin. Already we were defining ourselves as a people that spends an unnatural amount of time riding around on skates.

96

Many patriots claim that hockey is Canada's national sport but I think they're only half right. I think that skating is Canada's true national sport. It's nonsexist for starters, and besides, outside of beer commercials, how many fellow citizens do you know who play hockey past the age of twenty-five?

Nope, for most Canadians, skating it is. As kids, skating was what we did all winter long down at the pond for as long as the ice was sound and the weather wasn't too foul. We skated from the time we could sneak down our driveways in the morning until it got too dark to see the treacherous cracks in the ice. We skated too long—'way past the point at which our noses and ear tips were merely cold. We played pick-up hockey, tag and crack the whip while the cold seeped into our bones, and later we danced home on throbbing feet, full of fearful imaginings of toes turned black, trying not to sob because it *hurt so much* and our fingers were too stiff and clumsy with the cold to undo the laces, which were frozen solid to the skates, which Oh God! had to come off *right now*!

All this was quite forgotten by next morning, when, topped up with toast and Beehive Golden Corn Syrup, we crammed warm feet into those very same skates and clumped out the door, dodging maternal imprecations to "Keep off the linoleum!"

Going skating. Do kids still do it today? I don't mean skating in circles down in the bowels of heated arenas listening to scratchy sound systems croak out Rod Stewart and Tina Turner. That's not skating, that's Being in Heat. Those kids could have roller skates or disco boots or hot dog buns on their feet and they wouldn't know the difference. No, I'm talking about real skating—the kind that's been going on in the open air on Canada's rivers and ponds ever since some forgotten pioneer discovered the singular thrill of flashing over the ice on wedges of metal. I speak of the pre-Zamboni era, when the ice was flooded by garden hoses if at all, and it was kept clean by kids wielding snow shovels—whole squads of them, moving in tandem in a kind of flying wedge, their shovels angled just so, successive shovellers scooping up the overflow left by the shoveller in front of them. Nobody ever gave seminars or courses on how to do that, it was just one of the things you magically assimilated by going skating.

And, of course, there was love. Adults were responsible for

introducing romance into an otherwise innocent pastime. On our pond, I'm pretty sure it was the old Ukrainian couple who did it. All the kids snickered at them because, well, they talked so funny for one thing—and their skates were hilarious! Shiny black leather boots mounted on long skinny blades with lethal-looking points. What's more, they both wore long, heavy black woollen coats that kind of flapped when they skated, making them look like a pair of huge crows skimming the pond. But my, they could skate, and they held hands in a complicated way I'd never seen before—his arm around her back, her arms crossed in front of her so that he got to hold both her hands and to hug her, all at once. The girls watched them skate by and one of them whispered that they looked beautiful. The boys didn't say anything, but I think we all knew we were doomed. The seed was planted.

Maybe it was the Ukrainian couple, perhaps it was hormones thawing. I only know that it wasn't too long before the boys were going skating nearer to sundown. And we were wearing our best windbreakers and leaving vapour trails of Wildroot Cream Oil and Brylcreem. The girls arrived later too, in giggling gaggles that thinned out as they scouted the terrain.

That first encounter was as stiffly ceremonial as the rituals observed by a pair of whooping cranes. The Boy, whooshing up and down the ice, putting on his best moves, circling ever closer to The Girl. And The Girl, pumping along on the picks of her figure skates in little rhythmic spurts like a hobbled bird. She has shed her maids-in-waiting; he is ignoring his old hockey buddies. Everyone is aware that a courtship is in progress.

HE: [stopping in a spray of ice chips] Cold, eh?
SHE: Sure is.
HE: S'okay 'f' I skate with ya a little?
SHE: I guess . . .

All delivered in mightily bored tones, you understand, with the most elaborate casualness and studied nonchalance. Meanwhile, under layers of wool and cotton and sweat shirt and training bra, hearts flipped convulsively, like two bass in the bottom of a boat. Is there anyone out there so old and jaded they can't remember the electric jolt when those two mittened hands found each other in the dark? Ah, young love. Skating was such a good place for it to happen. You didn't have to buy tickets or coax the old man into lending the car. It was out in the fresh air, so it was healthy and, above all, it was safe. Parents must have loved that. Not much likelihood of hanky-panky when the mercury was down around freezing and under the spreading chestnut tree the snow was two feet deep. Besides, it would be April before anybody could get through all those layers of clothes.

Joni Mitchell sings a song about a dead love affair that contains the line: "I wish I had a river I could skate away on." I wonder if you have to be Canadian to appreciate that?

Once, for one day of one winter, I had a river I could skate away on. It was the Humber, on a stretch north of Toronto. The day was in January, I was twelve, and the mercury plummeted from well above freezing to well below in a matter of hours. The river, which had been chugging along minding its own business, suddenly froze into an endless mirror of ice as smooth and hard as a marble highway. I don't know how many miles I skated, but I skated all that day. I skated around bends and up creeks and through towns and villages I'd never seen before. I remember crawling into my bed that night on legs as shaky as slinky toys. My mother tells me that I passed out with a smile on my face. It was the end of one of the most beautiful days of my life.

The Russian poet Yevtushenko once told a reporter: "I say the best Canadian poet is Phil Esposito and that is not completely a joke. . . ." So who's laughing? Another hockey player by the name of Eric Nesterenko said it for all of us, be we hockey pros, Ice Capaders or just average droopy-ankled once-in-a-blue-moon skaters.

"Some nights you just go. You can't stop. The rhythm gets to you, the speed. You're moving, man, moving, and that's all."

Indeed it is. I may just have to go down in the basement this weekend and dig out those skates.

GOING FOR GROSS

THE HOLIDAY SEASON is upon us and I hate it. I have nothing against Saint Nick, mistletoe, or roasting chestnuts. I think I'm even ready to hear the Harry Simeon Chorale do "Little Drummer Boy" another 112 times.

No, what I hate about this season are the warnings on the label. The don't-over-indulge warnings: "To burn off the calories contained in one canape, you would have to scale the north face of Everest buck naked with two electric typewriters strapped to your back."

And the don't-eat-anything-that-tastes-good warnings: "Laboratory tests have shown that rats fed on a diet of bacon, butter, beer and brandy are eighty-five point seven times more likely to develop interstitial carcinomas."

And there's more. Participaction personnel wonder if I'm monitoring my cardiovascular system. The Liver Foundation says to watch the whites of my eyes. The police have made it clear that it's an economy suite at the Crowbar Hotel for me if I so much as glance at a glass of egg nog while jangling the car keys in my pocket. Which is fine. I am opposed to drunk drivers. I hold no brief for thrombosis, sclerosis, cirrhosis or any other diseases of sloth and excess.

What bugs me is that all these alarms are being sounded *now*. On the threshold of the winter holiday season—the most decadent and excessive orgiastic drinking, smoking and feeding frenzy we have.

100

Anyone hoping to pursue a course of discretion and temperance in these nether weeks of the year must cross a minefield of extra-long lunches, office parties and Wed-Thur-Friday night get-togethers for munchies and drinkie poos with people who wouldn't bother to swear at us the other eleven months of the year.

I can't take the pressure. And this year, I'm not going to try. This year I'm gonna go for gross. I'm going to pig out. Overeat, overdrink, oversmoke and make an overly large fool of myself right down to lampshades on the head and 3 A.M. falsetto renditions of "The Whiffenpoof Song." In other words, my usual Yuletide M.O. . . . but this time without the handwringing.

One last act of prudence. I'm putting the car keys in a padded envelope and mailing them to myself. I figure with the Christmas mailing rush and the Canada Post Year-End Holiday Schedule, I'll be lucky to get back behind the wheel before Valentine's Day.

STRANGE DEVELOPMENTS IN THE FIELD OF L'AMOUR

MARSHALL MCLUHAN MADE A chilly little observation in an interview he gave a few years before his death. He said, "Projecting current trends, the love machine would appear a natural development in the near future—not just the computerized datefinder, but a machine whereby ultimate orgasm is achieved by direct mechanical stimulation of the pleasure circuits of the brain."

A love machine. Well it hasn't happened yet, as far as I know. But there have been some pretty weird developments in the field of l'amour of late. Such as these bulletins culled from recent newspapers:

Item one: During the sixties we had a lot of "in's"—drop-ins, sing-ins, bed-ins, be-ins. Last week on the campus of the University of South Carolina they had a new one on me. A hug-in. Their Third Annual Hug-In, as a matter of fact. Students ran around all day clutching people and then getting their quarries to sign a tally sheet, attesting to the fact that they had been well and truly hugged. This was no bunny hop. The huggers begged, cajoled, ambushed and even threatened potential huggables in an attempt to fatten their scores. Object of the exercise: to hug as many people as you could in one day. A student by the name of Robbie Martin was the hands-down—or hands-around—winner. He copped 280 signatures, including those of four deans; the entire faculty of the English department; and all of the school maintenance staff.

Item two: I suppose it's not surprising to discover that spiralling prices have invaded even the wonderful world of romantic trysters. Why should lovers be exempt? There was a time when an amorous couple in search of privacy could rent a room for the afternoon—but have you checked hotel rates lately?

Which may go some distance toward explaining the odd sight that greeted the manager of Public Storage Limited, in Rexdale, Ontario, when he went to check out one of his rented storage lockers. When he unlocked the door he found . . . well, a bedroom, actually. Complete with bed, dresser, carpet and chairs. The fellow who rented the locker (ostensibly to store his boat) had in fact been using it to entertain a lady friend. And he'd been doing it for some months before he was found out.

But the manager was quite philosophical about it. "You can't blame him for trying," he said. "A hotel room can cost you ninety dollars a night. This guy was only paying us eighty-seven dollars a month."

Item three: Here in the Great White North, we Canucks do things differently, eh? Especially our perverts. Ask the woman who walked into a Winnipeg police station with a complaint that was bizarre even by Prairie standards. She told the desk sergeant that she'd been attacked. Could she supply a description of the attacker? No problem. He was dressed in a parka, with his face hidden by a scarf. That's pretty standard, but the rest of his garb was . . . memorable. On the lower part of his body he sported transparent red pantyhose and a pair of pink leg warmers. The man (if that's what it was) pushed the woman to the ground, then took off, without trying to hurt her or remove her clothing.

You know in a country like ours, where the winters are long and the nights are cold . . . strange things can happen—even to grand institutions like love.

Thank God spring is just around the corner.

FORTY IS NOTHING TO BE AFEARD OF

MY, THERE WAS A POIGNANT little item in the newspaper the other day. It was a story about a fledgling magazine destined to hit the newsstands next September. The magazine is called *Prime*. And its target audience—I SAID ITS TARGET AUDIENCE (turn up your hearing aid, for crying out loud)—is, wait for it now . . . people who are over forty.

By crackie, we've come a long way, old timer.

You mind the time that Bob Dylan fella used to sing songs about "the masters of war" and "the times they are a changin'" with the line that went "your sons and your daughters are beyond your command."

Well now, Bob Dylan never really came right out and *sang* so, but we all took it for granted that those songs were aimed at the wattle-draped jugulars of people who were—Gah!—over forty.

Forty! That was dinosaur-ville back in the sixties. Heck, there was a guy on the Berkeley campus in California who became famous just for coining the phrase, "don't trust anyone over thirty!" You bet! And we cheered him too, most of us being in our late teens and twenties and all.

You don't have to be Pythagoras or Archimedes to figure out that those of us who were in our twenties in the sixties find ourselves nuzzling our forties in the eighties. We are in fact prime candidates to join the subscription lists of *Prime* magazine, providing we can find our reading glasses, of course.

The fellow behind *Prime* is Douglas Squarek, and he's pretty excited about the venture. (Well, as excited as people who are fortyish ever get.) Of his readership, he says, "They are a very influential group." You said it, Doug. We're sizable, too. There are about nine million forty-plusers in Canada alone.

And we're starting to have some clout as well. Notice how the ads on TV have pretty well stopped trying to make us feel unworthy because we don't have eighteen-year-old bodies anymore? Advertisers know a losing battle when they see one. Nope. Now it's Preparation H and Jane Russell full-figure bras and Grecian Formula and denture cream and sit-down lawn mowers. The baby boomers have come of age. Middle age. We are thicker of waist, and shorter of breath; higher of forehead and flatter of foot—but we are the slice of the audience pie with the bucks ... and we *do* know what is happening Mr. Jones because we brought our prophets along with us. Bob Dylan is nudging the half-century mark. Mario Savio? Last I heard, he was an insurance underwriter somewhere in California.

A forty-nine-year-old insurance underwriter.

No doubt *Prime*, the magazine for people over forty is going to deal with the perceptions we have of middle age. Maybe it'll even have a "Where Are They Now?" section, so we can find out what happened to people like Jerry Rubin and Kahn Tineta Horn and Michelle Finney and Bruce Kidd and a home-town boy from these parts, Bobby Curtola.

Publisher Douglas Squarek claims the whole idea behind *Prime* is that you are not over the hill at forty. Hell, I thought the only person who didn't know *that* was Dudley Moore. Forty is nothing to be afeard of.

As someone once said, a midlife crisis is a lot like the army ... except the food is better.

I'M A
LATE-BLOOMING
MISTER FIX-IT

I T FIGURES THAT WHEN I finally did it, I would do it backwards. Moving, I mean. Most people migrate when they're relatively young and keen and sound of wind. I'm on the enfeebled side of forty and I see little *son et lumiere* displays every time I bend over to hike up my socks. Most folks who get hit with the major move bug go west—or at least north. I plodded south and east. The majority of adventurers opting for a new address are responding to the attraction of bright lights. They up stakes in Lower Sheep Dip, N.B. and head for Toronto or Windsor or Ottawa. I made my big move from the city of Thunder Bay (pop. 120,000) to the sprawling megalopolis of Fergus-Elora (combined pop. 8,000—somewhat lower when the Ex is on).   Sane wanderers hit the road when their farm gets expropriated or their jobs are declared redundant. I resigned from a union-coddled, piece-of-cake Crown corporation desk job with womb-to-tomb medical coverage, guaranteed pension, near-senatorial perks ... to flounder in the jungle of freelance journalism. A lady who got somewhat tipsy at my farewell party called me "brave." "Stunned" seemed to be the consensus among just about everyone else. I don't think it was brave or stupid. Just "backwards" like most other things in my life.

Now you take houses for instance. The one I left behind in Thunder Bay was a crisp, no-nonsense two-storey brick job with all those features an intelligent homesteader appreciates: front-door mail delivery, curbside garbage pickup, cable TV, calendar parking and a lawn so tiny you could keep it trimmed with toenail clippers.

All of which is fairly crucial when you're dealing with a person like myself. Which is to say, a klutz. Probably "card-carrying" if I could remember where I misplaced my wallet. Aside from being lazy, unskilled and mechanically ignorant, I don't even *like* inanimate objects if they feature moving parts. I consider them, well . . . uppity. I've got nothing against boards or walls or rocks that know their place and just lie around being boards, walls and rocks, but you give them a hinge or a pulley or an on-off switch and before you know it they're putting on airs and making you look foolish, square and utterly unrhythmical.

Which brings us, kicking and screaming, to my new house. It is in the country—which is to say, ungraced by sewer or sidewalk or water meter or cable TV hookup. In place of the old taken-for-granted urban sewer hookup I have a septic bed. Or so the real estate agent assures me. He says it's out there, looming somewhere under the front lawn, probably where the grass is the greenest.

I have never seen a septic bed and I don't wish to. I have visions of something out of *Dante's Inferno*, heavy on the purples and greens, and that's enough. Mind you, my sense of dread tells me that some day, with my luck, I am going to know my new septic bed intimately. It's another vision I have. This one shows me and my twenty-five-dollar-an-hour-plus-parts-and-out-of-town-service-charge plumber standing on my newly disembowelled front lawn, up to our gluteous maximi in . . . never mind.

Did I mention the word "lawn" back there? What a laughably inadequate appellation for the undulating expanse of prairie that surrounds my new house. No toenail clippers for this ocean of crabgrass. Agent Orange might work. Prescribed burns look promising. In the meantime I make these half-hearted pathetic guerilla attacks on the lawn from the back of a dwarf tractor a.k.a. a riding lawnmower. Yes, I know. I used to laugh at them too. Now I own one. The fellow I bought the house from threw it in as part of the deal. I thought it was a gesture of pure admiration for my Kissingeresque bargaining shrewdness. I now realize the guy was probably chewing his tongue to keep from guffawing.

Here are some things I have learned about riding lawnmowers:

they cost eleven million dollars each; have a top speed of two and a quarter miles per hour and break down every hundred and fifty yards. Oh yes ... and no dealer north of Richmond, Virginia carries spare parts for your riding lawnmower. Every *other* brand of riding lawnmower, but not yours. Here are some other features my riding lawnmower boasts: Power take off. Three point hitch. Hydrostatic drive.

I don't have the slightest idea what in hell any of that means.

Under other circumstances I might choose to go quietly gaga, just sitting and staring at my riding lawnmower. Luckily, I don't have to worry about that eventuality because there's no time. I have other things to worry about. Such as repairs.

You know how some folks put up those cutesy-poo, urethaned knotty-pine signs by their driveways? Signs that read DEWDROP INN or SHADY NOOK or ARNIE N' PAM'S BIDE-A-WEE? Well, I'm thinking of putting up a sign of my own, featuring a line from a poem by Yeats. My driveway sign will read: THINGS FALL APART; THE CENTRE CANNOT HOLD.

Neither, apparently, can the hot water tap in the kitchen, the doohickey that makes the garage door go up and down, or my roadside mailbox flap which, if it worked, would probably foil the foul-mannered fowl presently shacking up within.

As a city boy I never appreciated the dreadful regularity with which Things Fall Apart. Oh, it happened in the city all right— but it was never a problem. When things fell apart there, you just called Hydro or Bell or Maclean-Hunter or the super—or better still, old Mr. Wilson, the retired handy guy down the street. Life was so simple then! I had all their numbers scribbled on the cover of the phone book. They'd be at the door almost before I had the receiver back in the cradle.

Where I live now, one forks out forty-three bucks just to have the Bell van show up in the driveway. Cable doesn't come out anywhere near this far and I barely have neighbours at all, much less a retired handy guy like dear old Mr. Wilson, bless his horny, callous-covered hands. Well, I could ask Vern Pritchard I suppose. He's the fellow growing all that corn on a couple of hundred acres just down the road. But I'd feel a little foolish calling him down off his giant combine-harvester to ask him what it means when my sump pump goes *weep-a-chucka, weep-a-chucka.*

That means of course, that I have to do it myself. Here, in what should have been the easeful, mellow harvest years of my life, when I had hoped to perhaps breed orchids, and finally get around to reading the literary classics, like *War and Peace* and *Anne of Green Gables*, instead I am forced to absorb cruel truths about grommets and gaskets and throttle linkages and skinned knuckles.

But it's not all grim. I must confess I felt a twinge of pride when the sagging split-rail fence I bolstered actually stayed up through a pretty stiff windstorm. Thanks to my ministrations the eavestrough along the north end of the house is now doing what eavestroughs are supposed to do—channelling runoff efficiently and discreetly down the drainpipe instead of upchucking it all over the front porch as before. I'm getting fairly confident as a late-blooming Mr. Fix-it. So much so that after lunch I just may pop down to Canadian Tire and buy a set of jumper cables so I can "boost" the riding lawnmower. (See? I'm even learning how to talk handy.)

Nothing to using jumper cables of course. You just connect the positive clamp to the positive lead thing-y on the battery, and the negative to the negative. Red to red and black to black.

Or have I got that backwards?

UNCLE THURMAN

I SUPPOSE MY UNCLE Thurman is, by anybody's standards, a hick. He actually wears a pair of those old Gordy Tapp coveralls you see on "Hee Haw." He keeps his hair, such as it is, under a greasy John Deere baseball cap, and he drives a battered old pickup that's got so many holes, it looks like it's been operated on by the French Secret Service.

For eleven months and twenty-odd days of the year, Uncle Thurman stays out on the farm, which is a hundred and ten acres of Southern Ontario rock and bush and passable pasture land. In direct defiance of the province's egg, pork, beef, poultry, apple and milk marketing boards, Uncle Thurman runs that farm as he damn well pleases—which is to say he grows what he likes and sells what he can to whoever comes up the driveway. You want a bushel of unsprayed harvest apples? A jug of unhomogenized milk? A couple dozen fat, golden-yolked free range eggs? A side of un-di-ethyl-stilbestrolled beef? Uncle Thurman's your man. Can't give you directions to his farm though ... that would be criminal.

Anyway, as I started to say way back there before the sermon, Uncle Thurman doesn't get off the farm much, but for two or three days each year—be it for a doctor's appointment or some legal wrangle or the funeral of a friend, Uncle Thurman gets his best black suit out of the closet, flags down the Grey Coach at the end of the driveway, and heads into the city.

All of Uncle Thurman's nieces and nephews are delighted

when he goes to the city . . . because we know that when he comes back he's going to be full of great stories. Last time Uncle Thurman returned from the Big Smoke, he couldn't stop talking about "all the deaf people down there."

Deaf people, we asked? "Why shore . . .ya oughtta see 'em . . . all walking around with twin hearin' aids attached to big lumpy batteries in their belts." We explained gently to Uncle Thurman that those weren't hearing aids. . . they were earphones attached to personal radios. Uncle Thurman just scoffed. "Don't be so danged stupid boy! Who'd be fool enough to plug theyself into a pocket radio and risk gettin' creamed by the midtown trolley?" We had to admit that it didn't sound very sophisticated for sure.

"Nother thing I saw down there," said Uncle Thurman, warming to the role of cracker barrel raconteur, "damndest thing. Young folks luggin' talking valises around on their shoulders."

"Ah, those are ghetto blasters, Unc," we told him. "Boom boxes. Suitcase radios."

"You must be soft in the head, boy," said Uncle Thurman. "What kind of an idiot would risk a hernia totin' a suitcase around on his back just so's he could listen to a disc jockey?"

We allowed that yeah, it sure didn't seem to make a lot of sense all right.

"Speakin o' disc jockeys," said Uncle Thurman, "ya shoulda heerd the feller havin' a heart attack in the bus terminal— right over the P.A. system!" (There comes a point in Uncle Thurman's stories when you don't have to encourage him any more . . . he goes all by himself.) "Yep, he was announcin' the buses ya know —and doin a crackerjack job too: *GREYHOUND COACH NOW DEPARTING FOR* . . .—and then it musta jist hit 'em . . . a stroke, I reckon . . . cause it sounded kinda like *NOW DEPARTING FOR . . . LIZTOWONTASHAWANERAGGUERA FOWRS . . . DEPARTING ON TRACK BRACTEEN . . . ALL ABOARD PLEASE . . .*"

Uncle Thurman's audience was growing wiser by the minute. We didn't try to speculate on what had really happened at the bus terminal.

I'm even wiser than that now, I think . . . because I thought I'd better phone up Uncle Thurman and tell him I was going on the radio today to talk about his trip to the city. Well I called his number ... heard it ringing the usual ... two longs and a short. Pause ... another two longs and a short ... and then ... this: "Hi ... This is Thurman and I'm not home right now ... That means you could probably rob me blind, except for the fact that Pete and Agnes are home. Pete's a near sighted pit bull who don't bark but hates strangers. Agnes is a snapping turtle who wanders into the summer kitchen off and on. Which is where I keep the good silver and my petty cash, if you want to take a chance. Otherwise I should be home about supper time." Click.

That's the thing about dealing with Uncle Thurman. You're never quite sure which of you is the hick.

NOT KEEPING UP WITH THE SEXUAL REVOLUTION

I DON'T KNOW ABOUT you, but I'm feeling increasingly left out these days.

It's the sexual revolution. It revolved right over me. I think I've pretty well resigned myself to it now. I accept the fact that there are some erotic byways and cul de sacs that I will never dally along.

Things like rubber costumes. Shoe worship. Birch rods. Girls dressed up like eighteenth-century Alsatian shepherdesses. I just don't get it. Any of it.

Heck, I can't even keep up with the police blotter. There was a time when your run-of-the-mill sex offenders fell into fairly comprehensible categories like flashers and peeping Toms and dirty old men. Not any more. Herewith three recent "soft crime" stories culled from the newspapers—stories that tell me I'm not only not Where It's At ... I'm not even close to Where It's Near.

The first tale comes from Edmonton, where at last report, police were still searching for a young man who attacked a female store clerk last week. It wasn't your standard assault. The clerk, who worked in a downtown Edmonton shopping mall, told police that she'd been talking on the telephone when the unidentified male attacker, sprang at her. Sort of. What he actually did was lunge at her left ankle, rip off her shoe and bite her on the big toe. Then he scuttled away, no doubt to prowl the streets in search of other unsuspecting big toes.

Bizarre? You betcha. But what's really odd is that the Edmonton Police didn't think so. This was the third toe biting they've had in the past year.

The second story is sort of related—anatomically anyway. This story's out of Nashville, Tennessee. They finally put George Mitchell away. George is very close to what you'd call a habitual criminal. He had just got out of a correctional institute a month earlier where he'd served four years for the very thing he got nailed for. His crime? Footstomping. George Mitchell loves to stomp on women's insteps. He's been picked up more than forty times in the past fifteen years for footstomping. This time they'll likely throw the key away. May the Lord have mercy on his soles.

Our third story brings us back to Canada—to Winnipeg, in fact, where recently a provincial court judge sentenced a Winnipeg fireman to four years' probation for his off-hours activities— harassing female students at the University of Manitoba. It wasn't just the harassment—it was the way he harassed them. The fireman liked to dress up in pantyhose, pink leg warmers and various feminine undergarments, and *then* go out and bug the women.

I don't know ... toe biting ... instep stomping ... courtship rituals revolving around pantyhose and pink leg warmers ... I come from a simple, uncomplicated time, when introductions between the sexes were clumsy and bashful, but relatively straightforward. A time when even a hickey was considered *risqué*.

And if any young punk in the audience writes in to ask "What's a hickey?", I'll scream.

THE MARRYING PRODIGY

LET US NOW TURN our attention to the phenomenon known as Mr. Glynne de Moss Wolfe. Also known to his chums as Scotty. There are a lot of other human phenomena we could look at: Marshall McLuhan, Ghenghis Khan, Madame Curie, Farrah Fawcett, Mahatma Ghandi, Joey Smallwood. But right now, to the best of my knowledge, there is only one Glynne "Scotty" Wolfe in the world.

Scotty is a prodigy—of which the genus homo sapiens has thrown up more than its share: musical prodigies like Glenn Gould ... punching prodigies like Joe Louis ... scoring prodigies like the Oilers' Mr. G. But I'm pretty sure we've never had anything quite like Scotty Wolfe of Blythe, California. Scotty is a marrying prodigy. Or if you're of a more pessimistic bent, a divorcing prodigy. Scotty turned seventy-six last week. He also filed for divorce from Christina Sue Camacho, whom he married in Las Vegas just last January. Mr. Wolfe is taking the split well— and well he should. It's not his first divorce after all. As a matter of fact it will be his twenty-sixth.

Yup. Mr. Wolfe has forty-one children; twenty-five going-on twenty-six ex-wives, and a secure niche on the top of page 485 of the *Guiness Book of World Records* as the most frequently married and divorced human being this side of the harems and casbahs of the matrimonially unmonagamous Middle East.

Oh its been a busy seventy-six years for Scotty Wolfe ... and I don't just mean the twenty-six treks up the aisle. For one thing, Scotty has faced both ways at the end of that aisle. Mr. Wolfe is an ordained Baptist minister who has hitched his share of mooning couples, one supposes. And that's not all. Scotty Wolfe turned in a white silk scarf for the clerical collar. In his younger days he was a Hollywood stunt pilot.

I have to admit that I don't fully understand Scotty Wolfe. Oh, stunt pilot, sure . . . even the ministry. But marriage? Twenty-six times? Kind of boggles the mind doesn't it? Imagine having to go mano a mano with twenty-six individual legal beagles each representing a different sundered spouse. Imagine the writer's cramp from making out twenty-six different alimony cheques every month. Scotty Wolfe is a man who would know which month hath thirty days and which ones provide him with an extra twenty-four hours to rustle up the necessary cash.

And forty-one kids! Forty-one birthdays to remember. Forty-one graduation ceremonies to attend or come up with an alibi for —every year! Imagine the number of habits and idiosyncracies that Scotty Wolfe has had to get used to! Was it number sixteen that always had to sleep with the window open? No, that was twelve. Sixteen was the one who draped the shower track with pantyhose so that taking a simple shower was like an episode of Ramar of the Jungle.

Twenty-six wives! Twenty-six different approaches to eggs ranchero and pot roast. Twenty-six different mothers-in-law!

You know, you would think that it would occur to an ex-stunt pilot that being shot down on twenty-six consecutive missions . . . is an indication that perhaps God doesn't want you to fly, matrimonially speaking. But Scotty has not taken the hint. He's out shopping for wife number twenty-seven right now. And what about his latest ex? Scotty's already rationalized that one. He says the trouble with Christina Sue is that she was never at home. "These young women," says Scotty, "don't want to stay home and wash clothes and do the ironing and sweep the floor."

Well, you got that right Scotty . . . although cracking up twenty-six marriages just to emerge with that piece of intelligence seems like pretty slim returns.

Gives me an idea though, Scotty . . . when you tie the knot with wife number twenty-seven why don't *you* stay home and wash the clothes and do the ironing and sweep the floor? It'd be a change of pace for you. And at seventy-six it's about time you settled down.

MY DISHWASHER DOESN'T

YOU MAY NOT BELIEVE it, but you are reading the prose of a guy who never actually touched an automatic dishwasher until the summer of '85. Oh, I'd seen them in other folk's kitchens . . . maybe even covertly ran my palm along the outside of one or two I suppose . . . certainly I'd accepted the principle of automatic dishwashers, just as I'd accepted the principle of other great imponderables (death, gravity, the actual existence of a Toronto Maple Leaf fan club)—oh I believed in automatic dishwashers all right—but I'd never actually experienced one until just a couple of weeks ago.

This one came with a house I bought. "Good," I said to myself. "A labour-saving device." I've never been a back-to-the-lander—certainly not where used gravy boats, crusty plates, and scummy beer steins are concerned. If I can't have a live-in scullery maid (and my friendly Revenue Canada representative assures me that I can't have a live-in scullery maid) then I will cheerfully make room for a mechanical contrivance that does all my washing up in return for a few trifling ohms of electricity (or whatever electricity comes in).

Except that my dishwasher doesn't. Wash my dishes I mean. Not very well anyway. I stack them all in there, neatly . . . glasses on the top rack, cutlery in the little container . . . plates and saucers like grubby little grenadiers, row on row, bringing up the rear. I add detergent as directed, close the door and set the controls and push "on."

The machine lights up cheerfully. It emits a series of exuberant growls and hisses . . . time passes, the machine clicks off . . . I open the door to find . . . the same grimy stuff I put in there a whole cycle ago.

117

Actually that's a bit of an exaggeration. It's not that bad. Sometimes the dirty dishes are warm. Sometimes they're covered with a mysterious milky substance. Other times my glasses come back pockmarked with a grainy, pebbly finish that I don't remember ordering. And sometimes none of the above happens. Sometimes the detergent just transforms itself into a kind of oleaginous goo that bonds to the dispenser and has to be scraped off with the egg flipper.

I'm not complaining, you understand. I came, as I said, rather late in life to the phenomenon of the automatic dishwasher. Doubtless it's an acquired taste, like olives and single malt scotch.

I must confess I am a trifle curious though. From what I remember of the old prehistoric way of doing dishes—you know, sink full of hot water, a wee squirt of liquid detergent, a dishcloth, elbow grease—from what I can recall, that method *worked* for all its drudgery. Gave you dishpan hands but at least it delivered clean dishes.

And this machine is so damned finicky. Scrape off all the plates, I am advised. Rinse the glasses before stacking, I am urged. Don't risk crystal, silver, fine china, pots or pans or any vessels or utensils containing plastic, aluminum, copper or wood, it warns.

Well what's left? Near as I can figure, just that old fraternity glass ashtray that I haven't been able to get rid of in three successive garage sales. *It* comes through the dishwasher fine. Still dirty, but fine.

Perhaps the only virtue of automatic dishwashers is that closing door. It gives you somewhere to hide the dirty dishes so you don't have to look at them and feel guilty.

Remember Howard Hughes? He became rich by inventing a diamond bit for drilling oil wells. Remember Robert Ablanap? Another American multi-millionaire who made his bundle by perfecting the valve for aerosol cans. Our next tycoon will be the genius who patents a kitchen sink canopy capable of concealing all the dirty dishes, pots and pans generated by a typical North American family over say, two days.

I'd invent the thing myself, but I haven't got the time. Gotta chip this congealed detergent off my dishwasher before it hardens.

MY NOVEL NAVEL

I CAN'T PROVE IT, but I believe that Lyndon Baines Johnson cashed in his political chips by allowing two photographs to be taken. One photo showed LBJ hoisting one of his pet beagles by the ears. That took care of the animal lovers' vote. The other photo showed the then-leader of the Western world hiking up his Van Heusen to show a substantial presidential spare tire and what looked like a very short spur line of railroad tracks thereon. It was an abdominal incision. LBJ had had his gall bladder removed and was ingenuously pointing out the battlefield to delighted new photographers. The resulting revolting photo must have appeared in just about every magazine and newspaper on the planet. LBJ looked like a boor. And an out-of-shape one at that. Which is sad, because President Johnson was merely indulging in that perfectly understandable post-operative phenomenon known as "showing the scar." Unfortunately, scar flaunting is one of those activities better suited to schoolyards and locker rooms. It doesn't go over well in the Rose Garden of the White House.

Or on radio, for that matter—for which you can thank your lucky stars because if this was television you'd be looking at yet another exposed abdomen. I, too, have an overpowering urge to hike up my shirt and ask, "Whaddya think?" Not about my scar—although it's an unusual one. Your average appendix scar is just a neat, understated little whisker of an incision tucked off to the side, well under the bikini line. Due to complications, my abdomen features random punctures and clawing and a scar running

119

north to south which is not subtle at all. It looks like a plough's first pass over a fallow field. But I don't mind that. Anybody can have an appendix scar. Only a few of us get to look like we've been attacked by a psychopath wielding a garden rake. Which has its advantages. There is, after all, a certain ruggedness associated with scars. I'm already prepared for the blitz of beach bunnies who will no doubt circle around me this summer inquiring with awe, "Where'd you get that scar?" Which is when I mumble, "In ... in Nam. Look, could we talk about something else?"

No, the scar I can handle. The problem is ... well, my belly button. My navel. I think they moved it during surgery. No, this is no joke. I'm looking down at it right now and it is definitely lopsided. I don't think anyone should have to go through life with an off-centre navel, do you? Isn't there a paragraph in the Magna Carta about that?

I was getting depressed about my novel navel when I remembered that recently some woman in the U.S. took her doctor to court. He had promised her a sexy belly button through surgery. Instead she wound up with an eccentric belly button, like mine. She sued the surgeon for several million dollars.

Well I thought about all that, but I decided that in my case, before the lawyers got into it, I would call my doctor, drop some broad hints, and see if he cared to settle the whole thing quietly out of court.

For a man whose livelihood depends on a sharp scalpel, my doctor can be awfully blunt. He barked over the phone that it was not my *belly button* that was eccentric, and that to the best of his memory, my body hadn't been all that Adonis-like prior to surgery. But that if I didn't like the navel I had, he would be pleased to drill any number of test holes until we arrived at one I could live with. Then he hung up. Leaving me with a dial tone and my crooked belly button.

It's all right. I'm not worried. I believe in reincarnation, after all. I'll be coming back in another life. With my luck, as an orange.

DEAD LOVE

LOVE IS STRANGE. Love is blind. Love makes the world go round. Love is never having to say ... you fill in the blank. Lot of screen writers, paperback hacks, song lyricists and balladeers have had a few million words to say on the subject of love. It's been compared to everything from music to migraines ... from a red, red rose to a seven-year itch. Lot of nice things have been written and etched and sung about love, but there hasn't been all that much written about one aspect of the subject. You don't hear a lot of Petrarchan sonnets or Venetian gondolier solos around the theme "love is dead." But it happens. Romance dies. Some might argue that live love being like a burning flame and dead love being more like an uncleaned ash tray, there is perforce more dead love than live love around at any given time. And yet our legend-makers neglect the theme.

Not entirely of course. I think the famous actor and notorious philanderer John Barrymore was working around to a Love is Dead theme when he cynically and brutally defined love as "The delightful interval between meeting a beautiful girl and discovering she looks like a haddock."

Woody Allen is another casualty from the love wars who has given the Love is Dead theme a whack or two across the shins. Woody once said: "I sold my memoirs of my love life to Parker Brothers. They're going to make a game out of it."

And one more name that shouldn't be forgotten when it comes to the cold heart syndrome—Kevin Milmoe. Kevin is a twenty-eight-year-old law student in La Jolla, California. He operates a business on the side. He calls it the Dead Rose Company. The Dead Rose Company is predicated on the belief that there *is* something you can say to the ex-object of your affection after it's over. What you can say is: "Here!" and hand him or her a bouquet of flowers from the Dead Rose Company. A bouquet of brown, limp, thoroughly wilted flowers, tastefully wrapped in black tissue and bound with a black ribbon.

Sounds revolting at first ... but think about it. No whining phone calls in the middle of the night; no screeching, salad-throwing scenes in the middle of a restaurant ... no nasty letters of invective and recrimination. Just a bouquet of moribund roses. According to Kevin Milmoe, the dead rose bouquet gambit not only makes the giver feel better, the receiver seems to find the experience thought provoking and a bit of comic relief to boot.

All I know is that Kevin Milmoe's Dead Rose Company seems to have touched a nerve, if that's not a contradiction in terms. His biggest problem these days is finding enough dead roses to go around. Once or twice Kevin has even found himself buying fresh roses and then steaming them all wilty over a kettle, just to keep up with the demand.

Which proves, I suppose, that in addition to being blind, strange, lovelier and all those other things, love can be funny, even when it's going down for the count.

Speaking of count, I tote up observations on faded love from three people here—Kevin Milmoe, Woody Allen, John Barrymore. All of them jaundiced, all of them male.

In the interests of non-sexist broadcasting and equal time, I give the last word to Nancy, Lady Astor, who once said: "I married beneath me. All women do."

JUNK FOOD JUNKYISM

FOR ME, ONE OF the most humbling revelations that came with middle age was the realization that Newton was right. There really is a law of gravity. Oh, when you are a teenager or a university student you can appreciate the law of gravity intellectually . . . but when you reach middle age you can *feel* it, right in your bones. Or in the stuff that's attached to your bones. You start to sag. In youth we dreamed of "letting it all hang out." In middle age you have no choice. It hangs out all by itself. This is not true for some middle-aged people of course—the disciplined weight watchers. I have nothing to say to such people, other than that you make me sick. I have no desire to waste perfectly good mealtimes imitating a gerbil, nibbling at lettuce and gnawing on carrot sticks. Mostly I rebel against giving up junk snacks. That's the last petty vice I have . . . and as far as I'm concerned, a life without black licorice whips is a life not worth living.

That's my particular junk snack weakness: black licorice whips. Sure they're a little bit messier than Lifesavers and not nearly as slick as Chiclets, but nobody said that junk snacks have to be a piece of cake. Besides, black licorice whips look pretty good when you stack them up against some of the other available habits going around. Cocaine. Single malt scotch. All night no-limit poker games with gentlemen from Chicago who answer to names like Vinnie and Big Sal.

Nope, a passion for black (never red, puh-*leeze*) licorice whips is pretty innocent stuff—and certainly no less bizarre than some of the oral fixations vastly more celebrated people have fallen

123

prey to. Winston Churchill had a passion for great black cigars only slightly smaller than torpedos. George Washington probably would have surrendered to the British, if they'd had the foresight to offer him a lifetime supply of *his* favourite—candied almonds. The man who was in charge of the Manhattan Project—the scheme that led to the first atomic bomb—was General Leslie Groves. The General was an understandably cautious man. It comes as no surprise to learn that General Groves kept all the secret documents relating to the bomb securely locked in a safe. What is a trifle disconcerting is the fact that General Groves kept his secret addiction locked up in the same safe. The plans for the atomic bomb were held down by a box of the General's favourite chocolates—you know, those ones with the cream centres?

Other celebrity cravings abound. Hugh Hefner, founder of *Playboy* magazine, is hooked on Pepsi Cola. He buys it by the case. As does our own External Affairs Minister Joe Clark. And that is probably the only thing that Hugh Hefner and Joe have in common.

And, lest we be accused of favouritism in the cola wars, let's get it on the record that Duke Ellington loved Coca Cola—but only with a couple of extra spoonfuls of sugar in it. That is probably the only revolting thing I know about Duke Ellington.

Junk food junkyism is no respecter of sex or status—Queen Elizabeth the First virtually rotted her teeth out with sweets. Junk food doesn't much care about its victims' politics either. Gloria Steinem admits that every so often she goes on a bender and demolishes a quart of ice-cream, single spooned, at one sitting.

Speaking of politics, I suppose the most famous junk snack habit occupies a glass jar on a table in the Oval Office. Jelly beans. President Reagan loves them. Not just any jelly bean mind you—he goes for the black ones. On the other hand, when he was U.S. secretary of state, Alexander Haig (perhaps taking political symbolism a little too seriously) would conduct search and destroy missions to ferret out the red (natch!) jelly beans.

Wonder what they put out in glass jars in the Kremlin? Used to be vodka, but they're cutting back on that. Gorbachev doesn't look like a jelly bean man to me. Jawbreakers maybe ... or humbugs. There's probably a whole international junk snack protocol that you and I aren't even aware of.

Well, I don't know much about rarified diplomacy but I know all about sweet tooths. And I'd betcha a dollar to a jelly-filled doughnut that if we could just get Gorbachev and Reagan sitting down with a sheaf of black licorice whips between them, we could turn all our bomb shelters into mushroom farms. It's absolutely impossible to look belligerent with half a yard of licorice whip hanging out of your mouth.

ON BLOWING YOUR STACK

I WANT TO TALK about top-blowing today. Also known as cork-popping, spleen-venting, Cain-raising, ruckus-causing and handle, flying off the.

Curious, all the action verbs we employ to describe the phenomenon of hitting the roof. There is also blood-boiling, bridling or bristling with rage, lashing into a fury and blowing off steam.

And yet the most common cliché to describe getting angry sounds almost platonic. Lose your temper. "Oh, I lost my temper." Sounds about as volatile as misplacing a paperclip.

Ah well ... What brought on this musing on irascibility was an article on anger that I read in a magazine recently. The article was an excerpt from a new book called *Anger: The Misunderstood Emotion*. Author of the article and the book is a woman by the name of Carol Tavris. She works for the New School for Social Research in New York, and Ms. Tavris is not a spleen-venter or a cork-popper. No. She favours ... Well, before I tell you how she thinks you and I should deal with anger ... What would you expect her to say? I mean here we have a professional, a social scientist, with enough letters behinds her name to start a new language. She has degrees, she's done doctorates and theses, given lectures and has now written a book on the subject of anger. So whatever she advises is bound to be learned, complex, erudite ... possibly even incomprehensible to anyone this side of a staff member of the Clarke Institute, right? Wrong. Ms. Tavris says when you find yourself about to blow your top, you should count to ten. Just like dear old Mom used to try to teach me.

She says counting to ten has survived through the centuries as a method of dealing with anger for one very simple reason: it works. She believes any emotional arousal will simmer down if you just give it enough time, and, she says, venting anger can often make it worse. And Ms. Tavris has scientific research to back her up. She talks about one study that shows employees who reported an unjust boss to higher authorities had higher blood pressure than employees who simply walked away from a confrontation. Counted to ten, if you will.

Well, it sounds good, and I'm sure it works, but not for me. I've never got beyond the count of three.

About the only temper control that works for me is a half measure at best. I smoke a pipe. Whenever I feel my internal thermostat rising, I reach for my briar. Then I try to find my tobacco pouch. I rummage around for matches. As often as not, I discover that my pipe is half-full of charred dottle, so I have to cast around for an ash tray. So there I am with a pipe in my mouth my hands full of smoking accessories wandering around the room looking for an ashtray. I'm getting angry about something else you understand and I would dearly like to look like Charlton Heston coming down from the mountain. Instead I look like Dagwood Bumstead on a bad day.

But my old pal, Findley, had an even better way of handling anger. Findley was a merchant seaman. He sailed the Great Lakes. He was a short, stubby Scot, with red hair and a permanently vermillion complexion—all the clichés that are supposed to add up to "hair trigger" temper.

But they didn't. Findley was as peaceful as the Great Buddha. I've never seen him lose his temper. Never heard him even raise his voice. And I never understood it.

Not until I asked him about it one day.

I said, "Findley, you gotta get mad sometime. I worked on the boats ... you can't tell me that you don't ever feel like yelling at the bosun or the captain. You have to do lousy chores in rotten weather, sometimes risk your life, you can't tell me you don't get mad at your bosses once in a while."

Findley just smiled and said, "Och yes soomtimes I get errrrked at my employers. But I just put a price tag on it."

I asked him what he meant. Findley explained that he assigned a monetary value to every hassle he encountered. Some were forty-five dollar aggravations, some were hundred dollar jobs. Minor irritations were only seven-ninety-five. Then Findley would put a screwdriver and an adjustable wrench in his pocket and go for a stroll on the deck, until he found a piece of equipment the monetary value of which corresponded to the injustice he'd been dealt.

"And then," Findley said with a purr "Ah just unbolt it and slip it over t'side."

Don't get me wrong. I'm only reporting. I don't recommend or condone Findley's method of dealing with anger.

But he was the most peaceful man I ever met.

LOVE WHILE THE TAPES ARE LONG

HERE IS A STORY in Canada's national newspaper, the *Globe and Mail*, about a Calgary couple making love. Nothing terribly unusual in that. Happens all the time. Even in Calgary, one presumes.

No, what's odd about this coupling couple is that they make love while listening to their personal tape machines. You know the ones? With the ear muffs and the belt-pack? You see, the fella likes acid rock; the lady prefers classical music, but they both like each other. So they doff their duds, don their headphones and ... so on.

The couple was turned up by a psychiatrist at the University of Calgary who specializes in the study of the psychological effects of mass media on earthlings. He says the couple's preference for wired up dalliance is, "The ultimate isolating experience" and he's so alarmed he's embarking on a special four-month study of what those headphone/beltpack gizmos are doing to all of us.

Well, good luck to him. For me it's just another confirmation that there's been a hideous mistake in the heavenly computer and I was programmed into the wrong century.

Remember how we used to handle our need for solitude? We used to go for walks in the woods, go fishing, or if that was out of the question, you'd close the door, take the phone off the hook, and put your feet up.

Now, in the great tradition of our portaculture, you can take solitude with you. With a hank of wire and a set of earphones and

129

a little box on your belt, you can be alone in the subway; shopping at Sears; jogging; cycling; in the bleachers at the Grey Cup game.

People aren't going to come up to you. They can see at a glance that you're in another galaxy. Personal tape players are the latest socially acceptable way to say "get lost" without getting punched in the mouth.

Wear your handy dandy headset and you'll never have to give some stranger directions to the Royal Bank or tell him the time ... or even say hello.

In personal situations, such as the one the couple in Calgary are fond of, you won't have to mess up a great physical relationship with sloppy protestations and murky declarations of things like ... well, love, and all that.

I don't know. I keep having this mental image. It's a sixteenth-century pastoral scene. The sun is shining, the birds are chirping, the bees are buzzing. There is an apple tree and under the tree, a young guy with his arm around a Moll Flanders milkmaid. The young fellow, who's name is Chris Marlowe, turns to his companion and says, "Come live with me and be my love, And we will all the pleasures prove ..."

And she turns to him, bats a pair of big blue eyes, and says, "Could you keep it down? I'm tryna hear the Bee Gees."

PART 4

AUTO ASSASSINS AND TERMINAL TERMINATORS

YOU KNOW WHAT THIS world needs? It needs a brand new word, that's what it needs. A word for the act that I feel an overpowering urge to commit upon the coffee machine in my office. I want to murder it. But there's no word for machine murder. Mechanocide maybe? Thing is ... I'm not alone in my lust. A lot of people for a lot of reasons hate machines ... and not just furshligginer coffee machines that keep their money. No, lotsa machines—pay phones, computers, money changers, juke boxes, defrosters that don't defrost, freezers that do. The list goes on. Actually I'm Simon Legree when it comes to machines. If I had my way, machines would live in ghettos, sing gospel, and only be let out to cut my lawn or figure out my income tax. If I had my way, machines would be made of softer stuff so that I could beat them up, slap them around and kick them without fracturing my foot. The coffee machine for instance, which is, at this moment, impassively digesting two quarters, three dimes, and I forget how many nickels—all of which belong to me. Coins that I offered in good faith in return for a coffee black no sugar.

There is a printed promise right on the machine's forehead that suggests such a transaction is more than within the realm of possibility. Insert nickels, dimes or quarters, it instructs. Push button for your selection, it says. Correct change returned below, it promises.

To paraphrase Wild Bill Hickcock—bullchips. I put in at least two *times* the correct change, pushed every button I could reach without a crowbar or an Exocet missile. Nothing. No coffee. No change. No apology. The machine has the coffee and the money. I am left with murderous thoughts and dark imaginings.

And not alone, I see from two stories in the newspaper recently. I have a soulmate in an out-of-work forty-three-year-old fellow in Vancouver for instance. This fellow mechanophobe—a pipe fitter in better times—has found himself, like a million-six other Canadians, out of work. Things were getting a bit tight after eighteen months of no paycheques. The man found himself living in a tree fort in Stanley Park while he waited for his unemployment benefits. Came the day, our hero shinnied down his tree, hitched a ride to the pogey office only to be told that he couldn't pick up his unemployment cheque. Why? Because the computer had "lost" it.

Not surprisingly, the erstwhile pipefitter didn't take the news well. As a matter of fact, before the forces of law, order and decorum could prevail, he managed to dispatch three counter-top computer terminals by cuffing them off the counter and seeing how well they bounced.

And this other newspaper story. Out of Bellevue, Washington. Bellevue had a pretty good snowstorm recently. If you'd been downtown during that storm you might have witnessed the following little passion play—which the Bellevue Police swear took place. See? Here comes a car slithering and crawfishing as it tries to make the snow-slick hill. Inching up ... almost there but ... ZZZZZZZZZzzzzzzzzz. Stuck. Smoke rising from the rear wheels. Hopeless. Suddenly, silence. The driver has switched off the ignition. He is getting out, snow shovel in hand. But he is not shovelling snow. He is using the handle of the shovel to break all the windows in his car—right down to the no-drafts. Now he is taking out a revolver. Bang, bang, bang, bang! There. He has shot out all the tires on his car. By the time the police come the man is beating out a good facsimile of a Rocky tattoo with his bare fists on the hood of his car.

Well, I sympathize with the auto assassin and the terminal terminator. I'm not condoning the mugging of computers of the blowing away of Buicks ... but I understand. And I suspect we'll see a lot more mechanocides as more and more machines invade our lives to not quite live up to the advance billing.

As for *my* machine problem, I'm taking these two newspaper clippings downstairs and I'm going to attach them—by way of direct threat—to the coffee machine. And that machine better hope that I can find the scotch tape, because if I can't, I'm more than willing to use a railroad spike.

LOOKING FOR A GOOD IDEA?

THE GREAT FRENCH POET and author Victor Hugo said it best: "There is one thing stronger than all the armies of the world: and that is an idea whose time has come."

Well, the zipper was a good idea. So was the safety pin. And I like those screwdrivers with the hollow handles to hold the various screwdriver tips. That was a good idea. Some day I'd like to meet the genious who invented windshield squirters and tubeless tires.

Those are all nifty ideas, but none of them are exactly new. Try to think about the last time you came across a really good idea—yours or somebody else's. It's been a while, hasn't it?

Well, don't panic. It just so happens that I've got three good ideas I'm happy to share.

Here's one from an issue of the *Journal of the American Medical Association*. It says that doctors at the Baylor College of Medicine have discovered that an inactive person—I think that's scientific-ese for a slob like me—that an inactive person can get as much protection from heart disease as a marathoner gets from running . . . by drinking three beers a day.

That's a darn good idea.

Something about the beer increasing the level of high density Lipoprotein Cholesterol—I don't know about that. I do know that given the choice between humping twenty-six miles three hundred and eighty-five yards over gravel and potholes . . . or downing three cold ones, well I'm with the doctors at Baylor Col. of Med.

Here's another great idea of our time. From Walla Walla, Washington. (No, I didn't make it up.) A bill collector in Walla Walla by the name of Joe Fletcer has proposed an ingenious change for Washington's new state lottery.

Mr. Fletcer is upset with the very concept of lotteries anyway. He says they're a foolish, pie-in-the-sky fantasy, that suck in people who can least afford it. Some of them, say Fletcer, spend money on lottery tickets that they should be spending on basics. Like food. And therein lies Fletcer's great idea. Why not, he says, manufacture lottery tickets from pressed beef, pressed fruit, or even protein wafers.

Edible lottery tickets. Why not?

Speaking of worthless pieces of paper. I've got a great idea brewed right here in Canada. Concerning the Canadian Income Tax Act. One Lyman MacInnis says that the Act is a mess; and that with amendments it becomes more incomprehensible every year. Mr. MacInnis says that the wasted manpower and dollars spent trying to unravel the Act are enormous and he says 99.99 percent of Canadian taxpayers don't have a hope of understanding it. Well there's nothing new there. Any Canadian who's ever grappled with his income tax form knows all that, only too well.

What is new, is the man who's saying it. Lyman MacInnis is a senior partner in an accounting firm. He's president of the Institute of Chartered Accountants of Ontario for heavens sake! If Lyman MacInnis can't fathom his income tax return, what chance do you and I have?

Ah, but I haven't told you about the great idea here. It's not Lyman's—it's mine. Well if you wanna be technical I guess it belongs to the aforementioned bill collector in Walla Walla, Wash. The one who thought up edible lottery tickets. But as Robert Frost said, "any idea is a feat of association." Besides, who could live on an edible lottery ticket? Its like one potato chip. But an edible *Income Tax form* ... Ha! Last year mine ran to thirty-some pages. We're talking a three-course meal here!

That's it. My brainwave. A personalized *edible* income tax form for the coming tax year. A great idea whose time has come.

Oh, and if there are any Ottawa mandarins listening—Patent pending, eh?

LEARNING ABOUT THE RICH

I GUESS IT'S SAFE to say that money is a subject not too far from the forefront of most Canadian cerebellums these days—what with chronic unemployment, rampant inflation, spiralling interest rates and a Canadian dollar that's doing a fair imitation of a mortally wounded pigeon. Most of us have money on the mind for one reason or another and I'm not sure it's good for our complexion. Accordingly, Doctor Black's antidote: a stroll through the land of the rich—meaning the folks who don't have to fret about car payments, mortgage default, nasty calls from the bank or inundations of mail—the kind with cellophane windows and "SERVICE SUBJECT TO DISCONNECTION WITHOUT FURTHER NOTICE" stamped across the page in red capital letters. I wonder what the rich people are doing today?

Chances are they're perusing the Robb Report. That's a magazine that comes out of Atlanta, Georgia, and straight into the foyers of the homes of the ultra rich. The subscription list features names like Eaton and Bronfman, not to mention F. Sinatra and R. Reagan. According to the publisher, subscribers to the Robb Report enjoy an average salary of—sitting down?—$281,000 a year. That's U.S. dollars, of course.

Now, folks with that kind of paycheque stub in their wallets are not going to be attracted to a magazine full of garage sale notices or used car ads, right? Sort of right. A recent edition of the Robb Report did feature one used car ad—for Nelson Rockefeller's old Rolls Royce Phantom. Guess the Rockefellers are cleaning out the

137

garage and want to get rid of it. Two hundred and fifty thousand bucks ... and they'll throw in a mechanical fitness certificate.

But enough of luxurious reading—what about exercise? Where do the rich keep trim? Well those who don't have their own private custom-made gyms right over the billiard room, sometimes join clubs. Such as the Vertical Club in New York. It's knee-deep in broadloom and chock-a-block with shiny chrome exercise machines (more than 250 of them)—all equipped with digital calorie-burn-rate readouts. It's not expensive to join the Vertical Club—a trifling twelve hundred dollars—but you do have to dress for it. Gold necklaces and bracelets for workouts are in. "Sport jewelry" it's called. Cartier does a darling little bracelet for just fifteen hundred dollars that positively *glows* when you get a little perspiration behind it. There are "sport perfumes" recommended for the ladies and "name brand" exercise clothes of course—Reebok sport shoes and Elesse sweatsuits that retail for $325. Oh yes, and one more thing about the Vertical Club. Don't expect to join and get fit. You have to be fit ... before you join. The manager Tom Di Natale says, "We have no fat people here. People join other health clubs to get in shape before they join the Vertical Club."

Of course. So much to learn about the rich.

Pets, for instance. There's this divine restaurant that just opened in the lobby of the Beach Regency Hotel in Nice, France. Gorgeous! An art deco dining room, a fabulous view of the Mediterranean, and a clientele consisting entirely of ... dogs. Rich dogs, mind. The place is called Resto-Chien, and it offers full-course meals starting with diced turkey and pasta and finishing with a selection of fine French cheeses. I mean really, where else can you give Fido a gourmet dinner for just five to ten dollars? But remember they only have stalls for twenty, so call ahead.

But enough about reading, sweating and feeding the dog—what about a place to live? Something really special. You're in luck. I found a new property listed just this week. Actually not new ... it's almost eight hundred years old. Lindsmore Castle, near Dublin. Available right now. Sir Walter Raleigh used to live there. Fred Astaire was a regular visitor. His sister was married to the uncle of the Duke of Devonshire, who owns Lindsmore Castle. He only uses it about six weeks of the year so he has decided to rent it out. Sounds spacious—stands on an estate of two thousand acres. Roomy inside too. Plenty roomy. Two hundred and twenty rooms.

And you can rent it right away. Just $3,250 per week.

Ah, me ... It is a sobering experience to reach middle age and realize all in one day that one will never rent Sir Walter Raleigh's old digs, work out at the Vertical Club, take one's dog for a bite at the Resto-Chien or subscribe to the Robb Report.

Not that I'm poor, you understand. Far from it. I'm as well off as Henny Youngman, who once said: "I've got all the money I'll ever need. Providing I die before four o'clock.

WEIRD WILLS

I, ARTHUR BLACK, BEING OF SOUND MIND, DO LEAVE
... this rather morbid train of thought and take a look at the
subject of last wills and testaments from a lighter perspective.
More than a few weird last wills and testaments around. Take
Herman Oberweiss's. Herman was a European immigrant turned
Texas dirt farmer who died in 1934. But not before he learned the
value of a Yankee dollar and the foolishness of spending hard
earned money on high priced, legalese-spewing lawyers. Herman
wrote his own will. In pencil. It reads, and I quote, "I don't want
my brother Oscar to get a goddamn thing I got. I want it that
Hilda my sister she gets the north sixty acres ... I bet she don't
get that loafer husband of hers to break *twenty* acres next plowing
... Mama should the rest get ... I want it that mine brother
Adolph be my ex EC u tor and I want it that the judge should
please make Adolph plenty bond put up and watch him like
hell."

My Revenue Canada income tax form should be so straightforward.

I've been thinking about wills ever since I read about Trapper
Jack E. Smith in the paper. Now there was a character. Trapper
Jack was a three-hundred-pound beer guzzling Falstaffian drifter
who washed up on the shores of Gibson, B.C. a few years back, full
of elaborate tales about his adventure-studded life.

He was a trapper by profession, but he'd tried his hands at
other trades. He'd been a soldier in two wars; he'd written some

poetry. He'd trained lions in Africa; he'd done a few oil paintings. Trapper Jack had also done a bit of sailing ... with emphasis on the "bit." The B.C. Coast Guard hauled Trapper Jack off so many shoals and sand bars that they finally took his captains hat away from him and suggested in the strongest possible terms that he consider a life of landlubbering. That was okay with Trapper Jack. He preferred to sit around Grammaws most of the day anyway. Trapper Jack was a popular figure at Grammaws—which by the way is a pub in downtown Gibson. Trapper Jack would commandeer a bar stool there, among his cronies, spinning tales and sipping draft, and smoking. Damned smoking. Not only made him short of breath, it got him in big trouble, smoking did. Didn't he get kicked out of the hospital last year for smoking? Thing was, it wasn't cigarettes that Trapper Jack was lighting up. Hospital administration had some image problems with the concept of a three-hundred-pound, grandfatherly-looking senor citizen with silver hair puffing on a reefer. Trapper Jack claimed it was a recreational diversion he'd picked up during his days as a circus manager in Africa.

Oh well. It's all fairly academic now, because Trapper Jack E. Smith passed away last year of various and sundry complications arising from a life well and truly spent.

But Trapper Jack had a little surprise for all his buddies at Grammaws pub ... a surprise that just came to light a couple of weeks ago, when the regulars at Grammaws gathered for their constitutional Wednesday afternoon whistle wetter. When time came to pay, the bartender told them: "That's okay ... Jack's got this round." Sure enough, Trapper Jack's last will and testament (which took a year to probate, mostly because it was written on the backs of several cigarette packages) stipulates that each Wednesday afternoon at 2 P.M. in the beverage room of Grammaws pub ... the drinks are on Trapper Jack. For as long as the money lasts. So far it has lasted about a month—which is to say four rounds of drinks on the house. Nobody knows how much of Trapper Jack's money is in the kitty and his will states that nobody aside from the lawyer is going to know. Which is how it ought to be with wills. And with drinks on the house.

In any case, Trapper Jack's is far from the weirdest will ever written. That honour goes, I think, to Mr. Samuel Sanborn, an

American haberdasher who died in 1871. Mr. Sanborn left his body to science, but with a couple of provisos. His will stipulated that two drums—that's ra ta ta ta ra ta ta tah Ringo Starr type drums—be constructed from his *skin* ... and that the drums be presented to his good friend. The will further decreed that each June 17th at dawn, said friend would lug the drums to the summit of Bunker Hill and as the sun rose in the east, thump out "Yankee Doodle Dandy" on the drums.

Well, personally, I prefer beery largesse to snare drums that feature belly buttons—I like Trapper Jack's legacy way better. It's not a Wednesday and the sun is still way above the yardarm, but meaning no disrespect I am raising a styrofoam cup of CBC cafeteria coffee to the folks in Grammaws. Cheers, gang! And cheers to you, Trapper Jack E. Smith, whatever celestial barstool you're perching on these days.

LIVING WITHOUT LONG DIVISION

I DON'T SUPPOSE YOU'RE reading this, Miss Huff, but if you are, I want you to know that I am on your case. Now, you know who I am, Miss Huff ... and I expect you know the reason for the overtone of blood-simple vengeance in my voice. For those who don't know about our relationship, I should explain that Georgina Huff was my grade five teacher. I didn't much like her and I don't think she ever considered making over her will to me, either. I showed my affection via spitballs, passing notes and sporadic sabotage of the classroom radiator. Miss Huff counterattacked brilliantly. She sent me out into the world ... without long division. It's true! I never learned long division. Still can't do it unless I actually set up the problem in apples or oranges or tennis balls all over the dining room table.

I thought it was a tremendous coup at the time—escaping from grade five and Miss Huff without having to learn long division. I realized later that Miss Huff had really blindsided me.

Without long division you can't do square roots. Or geometry. Or algebra. Or trigonometry or physics or calculus. Or your income tax return or your Safeway bill or simple temperature conversions. For the rest of your life! Oh, Miss Huff, you got me good!

And all these years since grade five I've tried to hide it. Attempted to blend in with normal, long-division-proficient members of the community. I've avoided high school reunions ... deftly changed the subject whenever anyone started to talk about "school days" or old math teachers.

143

I was so happy when Canada went metric! I didn't have to feel guilty about not being able to convert miles to kilometres or pounds to kilos or Fahrenheit to Celcius. Now, nobody else could do it either!

Ah but it still rankled, Miss Huff. I still smoldered under the oxcart of ignorance you laid across my back. My friends were just *confused* about metric. I was an arithmetic illiterate. All these years, Miss Huff, I've owed you one.

And now, thanks to a man named Hughes Chicoine ... I gotcha.

Mr. Chicoine is a man who had more or less the same experience with a college photography course that I had with long division. He took his course and failed. Now, students in that position normally have two options. They could, as I did, just forget it and labour on, crippled for the rest of their mortal span. Or they could elect to give it the old college try try, again ... and sign up for the course the following year.

Mr. Chicoine has invented a third option. He is suing his school. For breach of contract. He claims the instructor taught him a different course than the one he signed up for. An Ontario provincial court has agreed that he at least has a case to make.

I think it's a delicious precedent, not to mention a rewrite of the old axiom. Now it will read, "If at first you don't succeed, sue, sue the school."

I don't want to be overbearing about this, Miss Huff, but I have spoken to my solicitor, and he says we've got an extremely good case against you. But, Miss Huff ... I'll tell you the truth. I may not (thanks to you) know my isosceles triangles from a square on the hypotenuse ... sines and cosines may just be so much Euclidean Greek to me, but I am sensitive to the quality of mercy, Miss Huff. I'll make a deal with you. We can settle out of court.

I'm willing to drop the suit and bury the hatchet if, come April ... you'll just take a wee peek at my income tax return???

HENRY SQUIRREL AND JIMMY COHOON, EX-MILLIONAIRES

REMEMBER 1985? IF SHE DID to you what she did to me, she was neither the best nor the worst of years. But for a couple of Canadians by the name of Henry Squirrel and Jimmy Cohoon, 1985 was both.

Henry and Jimmy started out 1985 about as flat broke and prospectless as you can get in this country. Henry Squirrel was knocking down about thirty-five bucks a week doing odd jobs and scrounging for beer bottles in the streets and alleys of Yellowknife. Jimmy Cohoon was chipping paint off an ore freighter in Thunder Bay harbour.

Then an amazing thing happened. Overnight Henry and Jimmy became rich! Demi-millionaires! They each won five hundred thousand dollars in separate lotteries. I don't know what you would do if you woke up to find yourself half a millionaire tomorrow morning. I like to think that after a couple of "yahoos" and a champagne breakfast I would settle down, behave maturely. I like to think that I would invest the money wisely and have it work for me. Henry Squirrel and Jimmy Cohoon are not like you and me. They had never seen so much money before in their lives, and they were reasonably certain that they would never see it again.

So they went for it. The cosmic blowout. It took Jimmy Cohoon seventy-seven straight days of hard-core, flare-nostrilled spending to get rid of his half a million. Jimmy started strong—withdrawing fifty thousand from his bank in hundreds—except for the thousand-dollar bill he used to tip the teller.

Then Jimmy *really* hit his stride. He went to a shopping plaza, climbed to the second level and began fluttering hundred-dollar bills down into the fountain below. Jimmy bought houses for some of his pals; cars for others. He gave ten thousand dollars to an old buddy who'd given him a place to sleep once—and as an afterthought, a thousand-dollar bill to each of the man's three children. In just two and a half months, Jimmy Cohoon was as broke as he'd ever been. Henry Squirrel took a little longer—four months—to get through his five hundred thousand. Henry seems to recall laying out fifteen thousand on "some German car" for some Alberta lady he met in the lobby of some Edmonton hotel. But the details of Henry's spree are even vaguer than Jimmy Cohoon's.

Thing is, while you and I were grubbing it out in '85—making the mortgage payments, stalling the guy at Eaton's layaway—Henry and Jimmy were saying: "Hell, let 'er rip! I'll have one of those and two of that for my friend here!" Sure they're broke now, but they were broke at the start of the year. And starting tomorrow, they've got a brand new year to try it all over again. Jimmy ... Henry ... wherever you are, Happy New Year!

And Good Luck!

TAXATION GOBBLEDYGOOK

JEAN BAPTISTE COLBERT knew what it was all about. He was a seventeenth-century French statesman who became Louis XIV's answer to Michael Wilson. After a few seasons of wringing francs out of his countrymen for the king's coffers, Jean Baptiste observed: "The art of taxation consists in so plucking the goose as to obtain the largest amount of feathers with the least amount of hissing."

Exactly. And that's the problem with being a Canadian taxpayer. No finesse. We don't get plucked, we get goosed.

It's disagreeable enough to ruin a Canadian spring by making involuntary contributions toward senatorial salaries, limo service for John Crosbie, and new cupboards in the Stornaway kitchen— bad enough to get dunned for all that, but . . . to have to deal with a Revenue Canada income tax form *as well*?

That's like being asked by your mugger if you'd mind filling out a performance rating chart.

Don't get me wrong. I am not opposed to paying income tax. I doubt that anyone to the left of, say Harold Ballard, is. I do, however, object to that preposterous sheaf of bookkeeping gobbledygook that we're expected to wade through before we surrender our ransom.

Turn with me now to page one of your Guide to the Standard Financial Statements, and savour the following sentence:

"The Income Tax Act authorizes the Department to reassess a return of income or make additional assessments, or assess tax, interest or penalties within four years from the day of mailing of either (a) a notice of original assessment, or (b) a notification that no tax is payable for the taxation year, or within seven years after the day of mailing of the notice of original assessment of a return to which a reassessment has been made or may be made to carry back certain amounts, such as a loss or Investment Tax Credit, from a subsequent taxation year."

That is a *ninety-seven*-word sentence which says—I think—that if your income tax return smells fishy, Revenue Canada's got between four and seven years to nail you.

Ninety-seven words! The Lord's Prayer only needed seventy-one.

What's really depressing is that this is the *simplified* Income Tax Guide—The Tory overhaul of the Mumbo Jumbo Doomsday Book of Horrors that the Federal Liberals employed to club Canadian taxpayers senseless each spring.

The truth is, I never get too far into my Revenue Canada tax guide, no matter who's putting it out. I always seem to founder and go belly-up around Chapter 4—completing the "Expenses and Allowances Portion of Forms T2124 and T2032."

It's right about there that I traditionally run out of patience and/or scotch, whereupon I cram every scrap of paper that looks remotely financial into a shoebox, staple a blank cheque to it and mail the whole mess to my accountant.

Income tax. A fair number of short-fused Canadians, from financial tycoons like E. P. Taylor to cartoonist Jim Unger, have fled the country just to get away from it.

Sir Harry Oakes did too. Sir Harry was a gold-prospector who struck it rich, then fled to the Bahamas to get away from the Ottawa tax hounds. Said Sir Harry: "I found the pot of gold at the end of the rainbow and I found it in Canada. But I was paying out 80 percent of the gold I'd found in taxes. Man don't work for that."

Indeed he don't. Sir Harry grabbed what was left of his gold and set himself up in Nassau, back in 1935. Eight years later he was found mysteriously murdered in a crime unsolved to this day.

But it bore out an old Ben Franklin adage. Back in the eighteenth century, Ben observed: "In this world nothing can be said to be certain, except death and taxes."

148

YOUR CHEVY'S A SICKO

OKAY, BACK OFF. Position's filled. This one's mine. I saw it first. Early birds and worms and all that. Don't even try for it. Besides, I've already got my application in.

It's a job. A cushy job. And since it's in the bag I don't suppose there's any harm in telling you about it. In brief, I shall be working in Washington soon. Big federal agency job. At the National Highway Traffic Safety Association, as a matter of fact.

It all has to do with car recall letters. You know, where car owners get a letter from the president of Stutz Bearcat, suggesting they bring the car down to the dealers so they can make some readjustments on the frameljammers connecting the catalytic afterburners. Well, car company presidents don't really write those recall letters. They have a fleet of attorneys to do that. And it turns out those guys are having trouble coming up with just the right wording.

When you think about it, that's a tricky letter to write. The letter has to be forceful enough to convince the car owner that he really ought to drop the car off fairly soon. On the other hand you don't want anything in the letter that might frighten the car owner into thinking anything is actually wrong, because that might lead to lawsuits and other unsavoury things.

Well the recall letters (there are anywhere from 150 to 300 recall campaigns in the U.S. a year) have been getting worse. The attorneys have been churning out recall letters that read like a Zimbabwean discourse on existentialism. Nobody could understand them. The owners of recalled cars were neither alarmed nor outraged. They were euthanized.

This is where the National Highway Traffic Safety Association —and my new job—come in.

The good folks at NHTSA offered to come up with a standard recall letter that all the car companies could use. They even hired a research institute—just to keep it professional. The National Highway Traffic Safety Association paid the research institute $23,008 to . . . well . . . to write a letter.

As you might guess, some headline-hungry politician—a Republican congressman from Texas—got wind of the story and whistled for the press. He got the TV cameras rolling and he asked a National Highway Traffic Safety Association official why it would pay anyone twenty-three-grand to write a simple letter. "Why," badgered the congressman, "didn't you just write a clear, reasonable letter yourself?"

Replied the NHTSA official: "I am not skilled at linguistics."

That's my man! That linguistically deficient management type right there, writhing under the TV lights. I got his name. And right about now he should have my career resumé right in his hands.

I included my price list: doodles $12; in colour $15; grocery lists $33.95; one-page memos $300; briefs $750 and up. Told him my full-fledged report fees ranged from $1,100 to $3,300 U.S., with footnotes extra—all with a money-back readability guarantee.

And just to show him what kind of a Can-do Canuck he'll be importing, I threw in a couple of Elizabethan recall rhyming couplets, gratis. Such as:

> *Please return your Studebaker*
> *Before it helps you meet your maker.*

> *You're chevy's a sicko*
> *Bring it in—we fix quicko.*

and,

> *If you keep driving your Ford*
> *You're in the hands of the Lord.*

O.K. it's not T. S. Eliot, but what do you expect for twenty-three, thou?

HEAVY BOLOGNA BULLS SOLD WELL

I HAVE A CONFESSION TO MAKE. I am a fraud. An impostor, a poseur, a pretender, a charlatan and a phoney. I am a two-faced fourflusher and a chameleon in ham's clothing. I've been faking it. Ever since I got into this business I've been faking it. It began more than a decade ago, my first day in radio. I remember it perfectly, threading my way through the crumbling ruins of tape machines and old announcers in Studio R, CBC Toronto. My downward arc of fraudulence began with the push of that microphone button. It will continue this afternoon when I push a newer, shinier microphone button and go on the air to fake it again.

The bald truth is . . . I don't know what I'm talking about. But let me explain. You see, this job isn't all fawning groupies and chauffered limos with tinted windows and chilled Mumms extra dry—no. I have duties to perform as well. I read stock reports. On the air. As a matter of fact I broke into the business reading stock reports on the air. My inaugural broadcast ten years ago went something like: *"And now, from the Ontario Public Stockyards, a summary of the markets to one o'clock. Slaughter steers and heifers brought a good demand today, canners and cutters were down, while good heavy bologna bulls sold well in mixed trading. . . ."*

I said things like that five afternoons a week every week for a couple of years. And I never knew what it meant. Canners and cutters . . . good heavy bologna bulls . . . mixed trading . . . any of it.

151

Time passed and I moved away from the Ontario Public Stock Yard Cattle Market Roundup. I moved away, but not necessarily upward. Today, a decade later, I find myself reading the Market Report from Wall Street. In which I read sentences such as: "Stock prices on the New York Exchange are surrendering some of their gains from the past three sessions ... the Dow Industrials are down ... in light trading ... and big board losers outnumber gainers seven to one."

What the hell is that? Sounds like either a front line report from some undeclared Latin American war, or the blow-by-blow commentary from a tag team wrestling bout. I have no idea what it means, but I go on the air every working day and say something along those lines ... trying my best to sound like John Beresford Tipton. Fraud, fraud.

But the stocks—live or Wall—do not represent my deepest source of professional shame. I can always console myself by believing that there are people out there somewhere—high priests of butcher hogs and sow belly futures—who can actually decode the garble that tumbles off my tongue. No, my real shame seeps from something else that I read with utterly false conviction every working day. The weather forecast. Every day I rip the wire copy from Environment Canada off the telex machine, dash into the studio, and pretend to tell you what kind of a day you're going to endure weatherwise. And I do it with mumbo jumbo like: ... low pressure trough moving slowly eastward will bring mostly sunny ..." or "a stubborn ridge of high pressure centred over the mid-west will give ..."

Does anyone this side of Percy Saltzman have any idea what that means? How about "variable cloudiness"? How fluffy is a variable cloud? How about "widely scattered showers"? Is there such a thing as closely gathered showers? And have you ever been out on a day when there were *one* or *two* snow flurries? Who's counting here? Or if it's Zen Concepts you're looking for, how about, "The winds are calm"?

I don't know what the humidity is relative to, or where the barometer fell from, but I do know this: I am fed up with living a lie and by God I'm just not gonna fake it anymore. I'm gonna quit one of these paydays and get into some honest line of work. Something I can believe in, like dope smuggling, gun-running, or

152

doing colour commentary for the Toronto Maple Leaf games.

That might work. "Well Dave, I think you'd have to agree that the Leafs put up a variable effort against the Oilers tonight. The dee-fence was hampered by broken conditions and widely scattered rushes, yet thanks to a low pressure trough in their own end they managed to outpoint the gainers four to one. Scoring as you know was mostly mixed during the third period but as always there was a good strong offering of heavy bologna once that buzzer sounded. I think in sessions to come you're going to see a wind chill factor roughly equivalent to unsettled market conditions in which . . ."

SOMETIMES IT'S DOWNRIGHT HUMILIATING

KNOW WHY I NEVER turned to a life of crime? Well, partly because I'm a chicken, sure. And partly because of all those mornings I spent squirming in the pews of St. Andrew's Presbyterian Church, I suppose. But I have a much better reason than that. I never became a criminal because I knew as a criminal I'd screw it up. And screwing up as a criminal is worse than screwing up as an honest citizen.

Honest citizens who screw up get fired, hangovers and maybe a divorce or two.

Criminals who screw up get busted kneecaps, cement overshoes and five-to-ten in Kingston.

So I passed on my chance to walk on the wild side, and every once in a while I spot a story in the paper that makes me glad I made the choice I did. Here are three such stories, all of which illustrate what I call Black's Maxim: not only does crime not pay ... sometimes it's downright humiliating.

Take the case of Robert Dean. He was an arson suspect under arrest at a New York police station recently. Dean, who was handcuffed, asked for permission to go to the bathroom. When he came out he had a big ugly .38 revolver clutched in his manacled hands. Well, the police disarmed him and Dean shot himself (not seriously) in the struggle—but the big question was: where did the gun come from? It sure wasn't in the police washroom, and Dean had been frisked when he was arrested.

Frisked, yes. But not thoroughly enough. Reconstructing the

154

crime, detectives concluded that Dean had concealed his gun in a roll of fat. His own belly fat.

Mr. Dean, who packs 250 pounds on his five-foot, three-inch frame, is recovering in hospital.

Things weren't quite as dramatic for a policeman in Lancashire, England recently, but just as embarrassing. Constable Henry Hitchcock was investigating a property damage traffic accident and suspected that the driver and passenger in one of the cars had "overindulged." But when he tried to administer a breathalyser test, the couple came up with an interesting defence. They kissed. Passionately. Obstinately. Inseparably. After two attempts to separate the clinching couple, Constable Hitchcock gave up. The dynamic duo didn't get away with it though. They were both fined for obstruction of the police and had their drivers' licences suspended for twelve months. That's okay. They probably prefer parking anyway.

Then there's the hard luck story of Martin Richardson of Victoria, British Columbia. Martin is not one of your big time underworld operators. No bank-heist, diamond-smuggling, million-dollar-cocaine-ring stuff for him.

And just as well. Martin Richardson doesn't even do petty crimes very capably. Not long ago, Martin was working overtime late one night in an underground parking garage, attempting to siphon gasoline from a vehicle other than his own. He even had a feminine companion along to act as lookout. In the midst of the gas-sucking operation, said feminine companion dropped her wedding ring. Martin—a felon perhaps, but a chivalrous felon—gallantly offered to help her find it in the gloom of the parking garage.

He flicked his Bic.

Martin is now recovering nicely in hospital. Victoria police think it will be only a matter of days before he is well enough to begin serving six months in jail and paying his fine of one thousand dollars for the damage he caused.

Personally, I think the only way to defeat crime is to nationalize it. Turn it into a Crown corporation.

That way we could be sure that it would never work.

UNEMPLOYED AHEAD OF THEIR TIME

ARE YOU LAID OFF, out of work, between assignments, on the dole, jobless or, as the current euphemism goes, underemployed?

John Farina has a word of advice for you.

The word is: "relax."

Mr. Farina is a student of the Canadian economic scene. According to his reading of the situation, the one and a half million jobless Canadians aren't economic casualties—they're ahead of their time. The wave of the future.

Mr. Farina says there's no reason to be surprised by the grim and ghastly unemployment picture across the country, because it's the logical and inevitable result of everything we've been striving to accomplish as a society for at least the last eight decades.

The man has a point. What are assembly lines, farm combines, snowblowers, computers and cuisinarts all about? They're about labour saving. Getting a machine to do the work of a human. Or preferably, a dozen humans.

For most of this century, mankind has devoted a goodly part of his energy to making gears, chains, cylinders and silicone chips to do the job that spines, thighs and biceps have done since man emerged, blinking, from the cave.

Well surprise, surprise … we succeeded. A simple computer nowadays can do in microseconds a job that took a whole floor of clerks a year to accomplish just a couple of decades ago. Think of a logger with a skidder compared to a lumberjack with an axe.

How about a ditchdigger wielding a spade compared to some of those colossal Euclids we see working on highway projects? Small wonder a lot of people find themselves out of work.

But John Farina says we don't have an unemployment problem. What we have, he says, is an *attitude* problem. Farina says the news media scramble around screaming that the sky is falling; the politicians scramble around trying to shore it up—and all they're doing is driving the rest of us to despair. Farina says we should be cheering, not moping.

He wants to see radical changes in our school system to prepare the next generation for what he calls "the new world of leisure." He wants to abolish all vocational courses for starters—why train kids for jobs that won't be there? He'd replace them with what he calls "social education."

What about the, ah, you know, the *money*? Where will that come from? Farina feels there would be no problem financing his brave new world where almost no one works. He believes "the new technology would enable the economy to keep growing." The biggest problem, he says, would be to find better ways of distributing the money.

That's where Farina loses me. Granted, my grasp of economics is shaky and primitive at best, but I never can get rid of the notion that money flows out of production, and that all production is a result—sooner or later—of human endeavour—be it brain or brawn.

I enjoy science fiction as much as the next person, but I just can't conceive of a world where machines bring in the crops, bake the bread, fix the flats, mow the lawns and fill out the income tax forms while the humans sit around in walnut groves, strumming lutes and taking lessons in advanced Urdu. Nice fantasy—but a fantasy, for all that.

In any case, for Mr. Farina, the whole question is rather ... academic. I said that John Farina was a student of the Canadian economic scene. He is also a full-time professor of Social Science at Wilfrid Laurier University in Waterloo.

He has one small advantage over the million and a half Canadians he is telling to "cheer up."

A job.

A MANIA FOR PHOBIAS

OKAY ... I WANT TO BE certain I'm saying this correctly: "Geph-hydro-phobia." "Geph" as in Mutt and ..., "hydro" as in the public utility, and "phobia" as in how I feel about going over Niagara Falls in a barrel. Yeah, I think that's it ... gephydrophobia.

Okay now, let me see ... I'm standing by the chip dip and she comes over and says something like, "Oh, I didn't see you come in." and I say something like, "Well, I didn't realize you lived across the river. Took me two hours to drive the long way around. I'm a gephydrophobiac, you know."

Oh hi! Don't mind me, I'm just practising a little cocktail chatter. I've discovered a brand new fear. Gephydrophobia. Ever heard of it? It means fear of crossing bridges.

I don't think I'm terrified of bridges, although I confess I have felt a little uneasy crossing some of the big ones like the Thousand Island Bridge, or Lions Gate in Vancouver. When you're several hundred feet in the air over swirling black waters—especially in a car which you know would sink like a stone—you can't help hoping that the contractor who built the bridge at least had an engineering degree.

Apparently gephydrophobia is a fairly common human afflic-tion. Out in California, medical experts estimate that there are sixteen thousand gephydrophobiacs in the San Francisco Bay area alone. And they are so terrified of bridge-crossing, they need medical assistance. Must be pretty tough for them, considering that the Bay area is a latticework of bridges, including one of the biggest, the Golden Gate.

Well, I'm happy to say that gephydro is no phobia of mine. I don't have any phobias that I know of. I do have a mania though —a mania for collecting phobias. A few years ago, the London *Sunday Times* reported on a survey of phobias. Fascinating reading. The survey found that generally (and Gloria Steinem notwithstanding) women were far more fearful than men. Twice as many were afraid of heights, bugs, deep water and flying. Three times as many were frightened of darkness; four times as many were frightened of elevators. The only place where men shone in the phobia department was in fear of financial problems.

The survey asked three thousand people one simple question: "What are you most afraid of?" The answers are interesting. Five percent of the respondents were most afraid of escalators. Nine percent were afraid of driving or riding in a car. Eighteen percent said flying was their greatest fear. Twenty-two percent claimed that fear of insects was what bothered them the most.

And what do you think was the greatest phobia? What would you guess most of the people polled, named as their greatest fear?

I would have picked fear of heights if you'd asked me before I saw the survey. But I would have been wrong. Acrophobia was a popular fear—32 percent of the people picked it. But it wasn't the biggest one.

The biggest one—named by 41 percent as the thing that terrified them most—was speaking before a group.

Hm.

Strange.

Speaking before a group. Heh. I (ahem) never. Really. Thought about it ... but (ahem) that's sort of ... what I'm doing right now, isn't it?

(Ahem) Well, I have to run now. Yes, well ... Back next week? Oh, I, ah, don't know if I'll be back next week or not ... I'll cross that bridge when I come to it.

OH, GOOD GRIEF

I TRUST YOU'LL FORGIVE ME if it takes a little longer to get the old Olivetti revved up and humming today. Fact is, I'm labouring under a bit of a handicap. My mind (such as it is) isn't on my work. It is still locked in a death struggle, grappling with the revelation that Charlie has turned thirty-five.

Charlie Brown, I mean. You know—the fat, bald, worried-looking little kid in the sweater with the zig-zag stripe? Star of "Peanuts"—the most popular comic strip in the world? Yep, that's the one. Thirty-five years old.

Not that it hasn't been a satisfying run for Chuck. Born in a mere seven newspapers three and a half decades ago, Charlie Brown and the whole Peanuts gang have blossomed into a major globe-spanning multinational industry. At last count, the strip was carried by—wait for it—two *thousand* and forty newspapers in North and South America, not to mention Europe and Australia. Even kids in Japan know all about Snoopy's Walter Mitty-ish escapades, Lucy's waspishness and Charlie's traditional lack of luck with footballs, kites and life in general.

The success story isn't limited to the comic strip. There are books, record albums, tapes and Charlie Brown TV specials keyed to just about every holiday on the calendar.

After which come the merchandising spinoffs—Charlie Brown lunchpails ... Charlie Brown T-shirts ... Charlie Brown pencil sharpeners and wagons and soccer balls and sweat suits and ... well, just about anything that will stay still long enough to plant a Charlie Brown stencil on it.

Not an unimpressive record to rack up in a mere thirty-five years.

The irony is, Charlie Brown has always looked at *least* thirty-five—and more like fifty. Aside from Henry (a comic strip character only Neanderthals like me remember), Charlie Brown is the only middle-aged-looking cartoon kid I know. He wears a perpetually mournful expression that fairly groans of disappointment, disenchantment and despair. Finally, time has caught up to the face Charlie Brown was born with.

Thirty-five years. What's jarring for me is that I can remember when Charlie Brown and his gang first elbowed their way into my consciousness and it doesn't seem like anything close to thirty-five years back. More like . . . oh, say, four or five years ago. Ten, tops. But I guess that's the way it is when you grow, ah, more mature. The past starts to telescope on you. Things that happened twenty or thirty years ago feel like they took place yesterday.

Meanwhile you can't remember what you did with the car keys.

It's a sobering experience to poke around with memories and discover how fast time passes. Remember when the Russians shot down a U2 spy plane and made an obscure American pilot by the name of Francis Gary Powers world-famous?

Remember that famous quiz show "The Sixty-Four-Thousand-Dollar Question"—and the scandal when someone blew the whistle and we all learned the show was rigged?

Remember being one of the eight million North Americans who parked themselves in front of their TV sets to watch two U.S. presidential hopefuls by the name of Richard Nixon and John Kennedy square off in probably the most famous series of debates in television history?

Can you remember all those things? Well, believe it or not, they all happened more than a quarter of a century ago, back in 1960. Charlie Brown was just moving into adolescence.

Ah, time. The late Ben Hecht called it "a circus always packing up and moving away." I just wish it didn't move quite so fast.

I leave you with another sobering reminder of the headlong gallop of time: someone you know became a grandfather recently. Nope, wasn't me. It was a Liverpool lad by the name of Richard Starkey.

Grandpaw Ringo? As a middle-aged kid I know might say, "Oh, good grief."

HURT YOUR FOOT, ART?

ONE OF THE WONDERFUL things about working in radio is that you don't have to dress up for it. You sound just as good—or bad—whether you're wearing a T-shirt or a tuxedo. A corollary of that, I suppose, is that you don't have to be particularly "fit" to go on the air. And that's "fitting" for me today because even though it doesn't show on the radio I am not 100 percent A-1 prime beef on the hoof today. There's a distinct lurch in my gate.

It's my latest injury. As a certified card-carrying Clumsy Guy I get my share of them.

I've always been partial to the glamorous injuries. The ultimate, I guess, being the one that used to show up in westerns. You know ... darkness has fallen in Commanche country ... the few surviving cavalrymen are hunched around a tiny campfire ... one is groaning, another is sterilizing his bowie knife in the flames. One with the knife turns to the one with the arrow in his thigh and says: "Better grab yersef a bullet tuh baht on Billy ... this is gonna hurt some."

Now that's a glamorous wound ... Commanche arrow in the thigh. So are muscle pulls, leg sprains and welts on the cheekbone. I can see Jean Paul Belmondo or Harrison Ford getting a lot of cinematic mileage out of a welt on the cheekbone.

I don't get wounds like that. I tend more toward the non-sexy afflictions: stye in the eye, cold sores, heat rash. When I was a kid it was my friends who copped the exotic strains—scarlet fever, German measles. I came down with ingrown hairs and chicken pox.

I had always sort of secretly hoped, that with maturity would

162

come a certain subtle mellowing of my infirmities—a tilt toward more classical, even vintage ailments. Uh uh. It's been post nasal drip and water on the knee all the way. Last Friday night I picked up my latest. Scrambling off the Grey Coach from Toronto, breezing into the bus terminal, already laying schemes for a weekend's enjoyment. Fondling two tickets to a street dance Saturday night, thinking ahead to an afternoon Dads and Lads soccer match, I grabbed the big aluminum bus terminal door, swung it wide and ... ARRRRGGGH! Hoo Hoo. Down there. My right foot. I smashed my own damned stupid foot in the door! A minor embarassment and a bad bruise at worst for anyone wearing a nice, sensible pair of steel-toed army boots. I was wearing open-toed sandals.

Basically, it was my second toe—the long skinny one?—that took the brunt of the encounter. Bare toes aren't built for sudden, violent meetings with heavy aluminum doors. My toe lost the match. Quite decisively.

There was a fair bit of blood, and a great deal of hopping about, one-footed, and more than a little off-colour commentary. None of which altered the dreary fact that I had yet another entry for my "dumb injury" list.

There is a bright side to the whole thing I suppose. The incident has forced me to ... reassess the significance of toes in the cosmic wholeness of things. My ears perk up now when I hear what previously were throw-away phrases like "toeing the mark," "going toe to toe" with somebody, or stars "dancing heel and toe." I've even found myself thinking quite a bit about that second toe itself. Never realized before that it was actually longer than the big toe. Or that it was so densely packed with nerve endings.

On the down side, as they say, is the fact that, due to swelling, tenderness and the need to accommodate bandages, I still can wear only sandals. Which means that everybody I meet takes one look at the swaddled-up digit looming out of my sandal and says, "Hi Art, say, hurt your foot?" And I have to tell once again the depressing saga of Terminal Door Versus Second Toe.

Ah, well ... shouldn't complain I suppose—but it does get tedious. Tell you what. I'll make a deal. Next time we meet, if you agree not to mention my limp, I promise I'll ask you about your duelling scars.

COMPUDAZE

WE HAVE THIS BRAND NEW machine at work that can send your grocery list thousands of miles in a matter of seconds. But *exactly* your grocery list. Doodles, scribbles and all. No kidding. A little plaque on the front of this thing reveals that it is officially a Digital Facsimile Transceiver. Around the office we just call it "the new thing in the hall." Way it works, you walk up to it, insert your grocery list or any other document or even a photograph—into a kind of a tray; punch a few buttons, whistle a few bars of "Stayin' Alive" . . . and hey presto—somebody of your choice thousands of miles away is perusing your grocery list. Or whatever. It really delivers. We phoned to check.

I haven't a clue how "the new thing in the hall" actually works. I just did what I do with all dramatic technical innovations. I got the guy with the briefcase, who came to explain the machine, to write down the sequence of buttons that I have to push. Then I put it out of my mind. For a while. The other morning I was lying in bed, thinking about "the new thing in the hall," and it occurred to me that I've been doing that with more and more things in my life—learning the button sequence I mean. I hardly ever ask how things work anymore.

There was a time when I actually had a rough idea of what went on under the hood of my car. Oh, I wasn't into grinding valves or swapping headgaskets, but I knew how to stop a stuck horn, even how to take out a spark plug. Have you peeked under your hood lately? All those humming little modules encased in plastic and metal—looks like a set from *Star Wars* in there. I'm not about to mess with that. I don't think anybody is, this side of Isaac Asimov.

164

Other entire sectors of my limited expertise have been similarly erased. Typewriters. I used to change typewriter ribbons. Used to know all kinds of tricks—how to get around the holes in a well-used ribbon, how to take a ribbon out and reverse it so you got a few hundred extra miles. Not anymore. Typewriter ribbons come in chaste, impenetrable, shiny cassettes now. If it fouls up, you chuck it out and insert a new one.

Lawnmowers, same thing ... furnaces, same thing. My dad had a great cast-iron, hydra-headed basement troll of a furnace that thrumbled and shuddered and you had to kick start it. Really. If it didn't work you just went downstairs and put the boots to it. Right now in *my* cellar there's this svelte, brushed metal, suitcase-size box in electric blue. When it fouls up a light goes on to remind me to phone my Home Comfort man.

And banks. Stephen Leacock started one of his funniest stories with this sentence, "When I go into a bank, I get nervous." Leacock was talking about old banks. You know—the ones with the vaulted ceilings and quill pens and glass inkwells and brass wickets. Can you imagine poor Leacock in a modern bank—with Muzak and fluorescence and cardboard cutouts of Anne Murray grinning down at him?

How would Leacock handle a teller, with a purple forelock and a safety pin in her earlobe, informing him that there is currently no earthly record of his financial solvency because "the computers are down."

Down where? Whatever happened to ballpoints and appositional thumbs?

Yeah, banks. They're the worst. They made Leacock nervous ... they make me something more desperate than that.

Wanna know the most poignant capsule comment I've found about this confusing part of the twentieth century? It doesn't come from a speech by Martin Luther King or a poem by T. S. Eliot or a song by Bruce Cockburn or a video by Leonard Cohen. It comes from an article in *Life* magazine. The plaintive cry of some poor little bank customer in Lexington, Mass.—so anonymous that the *Life* reporter didn't even get his name. Nameless or not, the man's words ring, "Our bank has one last living teller," he moans, "and I still don't know how to work the machines."

Amen, brother.

WILD
EXCUSES FOR
SPEEDING

THIS IS KIND OF A personal question but ... how do you handle cops? When they pull you over, I mean? I'm not very good at it. Of course I suppose it's reasonable to feel like the cat's got your tongue when you're conversing with a steely-eyed gent who happens to have a .38 Smith and Wesson on his hip, but I'm *really* not good at it. Even when I'm not guilty of impaired driving or going through a stop sign or failing to yield or whatever I'm being pulled over for.

Once upon a time I used to have coffee with a cop in downtown Toronto. He was an easy going, young guy with a wry sense of humour and a pretty good perspective on himself and the job he was doing. I remember one morning joking about getting pulled over and he suddenly turned ... *not* so easy going. His eyes got real hard and flat like Clint Eastwood's in a spaghetti western.

"What I hate," he said, "are all the ways you drivers try to con us." It was the way the drivers talked *down*, he said. The way they seemed to automatically assume that anybody is smart enough to outwit a dumb flatfoot. Nobody ever feels bad, he said, about lying to a cop. And when the lies don't work, they often turn to abuse and contempt and even threats.

"Every driver seems to have a brother-in-law who's the desk sergeant," mused the cop. "If I had a dollar for every driver who swore he'd have my badge lifted ... well, I wouldn't be sitting here drinking coffee."

I wish he hadn't told me all that, the cop. I was guilty of just about everything he said, short of the brother-in-law desk ser-

166

geant. I hadn't thought of that. But the next time I got stopped, I was twice as bad.

I've exhausted the possibilities of fake humility. "Officer, I realize you're doing your job and klutzes like me don't make it easier. I swear it won't happen again." He gives me a ticket.

I've tried fake outrage. "Now see here, Officer, you know and I know that nobody in their right mind comes to a full halt at a stop sign in the middle of the country." Ticket.

I've tried bribery. "By golly your right that is a twenty-dollar bill folded in over my ownership." Ticket.

And I've tried fake cameraderie. "Say weren't you and your lovely wife at the policeman's ball I spoke at last spring?" Another ticket.

One time I was tootling down the highway on my way home from work . . . a few . . . miles over the speed limit, I guess. I heard the familiar banshee wail, checked the mirror and saw the old cherries popping at me. Aw boy. Nailed again. What'll I use this time?

And it came to me. In a flash. Like Saul during his commute to Damascus. No excuses this time! I will tell, by God, the truth.

I got out of the car feeling like the guy on "100 Huntley Street" looks. "Officer," I beamed, "you got me fair and square. I was speeding. I would estimate that I was doing between five and ten miles over the speed limit. You have every right to give me a ticket and I expect one. I smiled. And waited. He gave me a ticket. For doing fifty in a thirty. Plus a summons for a faulty taillight.

Which leads inevitably to a news story out of Indianapolis. A story told by speed trap operator Lee Hyland of the Marion County Sheriff's Office, Indiana. He told of stopping a speeder who went through his trap at a very high rate of speed. He confronted the driver, who said (now listen, this is good)—the driver told the cop that he had been preoccupied trying to kill a bee that was flying around his car, and that, "My foot must have pushed the gas pedal down a little too much." He even produced the dead bee.

Isn't that good? Would you have thought of that? Unfortunately Lieutenant Lee Hyland of the Marion County Sheriff's Office is nobody's fool. He asked to see the bee a little closer. The bee, he noted, had dust on its wings.

"This bee had been dead for months," says Lieutenant Hyland, "the man kept it on his dashboard in case he ever got stopped."

The driver got a ticket. Lieutenant Hyland won first prize in the "Wildest Excuse for Speeding Contest," sponsored by the Police League of Indiana. First prize: a hand-held police radar scanner. Moral: if you're driving through Marion County, Indiana, drive carefully.

And if you must speed a little, be sure to dust your bee.

GREAT MOMENTS IN THE BAR

SOMETIMES WHEN I GET weary of the writing business, I fantasize about returning to one of my previous labour incarnations. I've got lots to choose from. I've been a movie extra and a sheet metal apprentice; I've herded cattle at the stock yards, loaded trucks in a food terminal, taught English and unclogged drains; I've sprayed paint on to the walls of school gymnasiums and I've chipped paint off the decks of an oil tanker; I've acted as a tour guide and I've stooked hay ... and I've sold: encyclopedias, men's wear, newspaper advertising. For most of those jobs, once in a lifetime is more than ample ... and time has not rosied my assessment. But there is one job from my past that beckons alluringly every once in a while. It was a job I held down when I was working my way through—okay, half way through—college. Okay, not college—Ryerson Polytechnic in Toronto.

The job was bartending. Yup, I tended a bar in downtown Toronto for ... I guess the best part of two years. I was a curly-haired, apple-cheeked innocent of eighteen summers when I started. I had grown up, for the most part, in the suburbs. Leave-It-To-Beaver country where everybody washed their cars and clipped their lawns and smiled a lot and voices were only raised in songs around the barbecue or if some kid on the school team hit a home run. And I went from that Ozzie-and-Harriet land to a bar in downtown Toronto.

It was educational. Multiculturally enlightening. The head bartender, for instance, was Gus the Greek. "BRRRINGUE ME TWO CAYSA FEEFTEY, WAN AH CANADEEN, A CASE

OFF EGGSPORT Den SHADDAPAH DOAN BODDAH ME."

That was Gus the Greek's standard sign-off. You knew the message was complete when he got to Shaddapa Doan Boddah Me! For him it was Roger, Ten Four Over and Out.

Then there was Eddy the Arab. He was the head bouncer. And he was actually Polish. I saw his paystub once. But he looked like something left over from the stampede scene in *Lawrence of Arabia*. Besides he carried a long curved Omar Sharifian knife in his cummerbund. Just for show, as far as I know.

I suppose all this doesn't make bartending sound all that wonderful, but it had its moments. It was a thrill for instance, after working there for a few months to have a waiter come up to you at the service bar, slam down his tray and bark: "Two CCs one VO, a rusty nail with a lime twist and a Guinness off the shelf." And to see almost like in a movie both your hands shoot out to fill the order. I learned to pour perfect shots. With both hands. At once.

I learned to mix fairly decent margueritas and Manhattans and martinis—and to wonder why so many mixed drinks start with M. On a really good night, Gus would leave the odd Singapore sling or lady's slipper to me—but not the really tricky ones. Nope, when the order came in for an angels kiss or a pousse cafe (which are more architecturally stunning than they are pleasing to the palate) well, that was the province of Gus the Greek who would shoulder me aside with a "Brrrringuh da Kaluah outta my way shaddop doan boddah me."

I remember great moments in the bar. The time we just about had a full-scale brawl on our hands. A big meaty, mean-mouthed drunk kicking tables and chairs aside, wading after another guy. He should've noticed Nick—the waiter standing just off his starboard quarter. Nick settled everything by raising his steel drink tray in a great two-handed overhead arc and bringing it down on the berserker's head. Sounded like Big Ben striking one. Could always spot Nick's drink tray after that. It was the one with a skull sized mesa in the middle.

Then there was the rat. Our bar had a giant rat. Greenhorns seeing it for the first time insisted it was a small dog, but old timers who knew better said no, it was a rat all right. Just an uncommonly large one, is all.

The rat didn't show up all that often, but when it did, it was usually a Saturday night when the place was packed. I wasn't crazy about the rat, but there was one waiter who was absolutely terrified of him. Harry. Hadn't seen the rat, you understand, but just knew he was going to, one night.

He was right. I was there when it happened. Harry was whistling across the floor with a full tray of drinks balanced on his palm, rounded a table ... and there dead ahead, he saw two little yellow eyes in a big swatch of brown fur. Harry went into a Flintstone skid. The tray of drinks went into orbit. Harry shrieked and jumped for the highest ground he could find on short notice, wrapping his arms around a pole and clinging for dear life. Regrettably for Harry, the Pole he wrapped his arms around was Eddy the Arab's neck.

Ah yes. The rat. Eddy the Arab ... Gus the Greek ... "Gimme two CCs a VO, one rusty nail with a lime twist and a Guinness off the shelf ..."

Yup. Whenever I get sick of the writing business I think back to the good old days, tending bar. Makes this business seem like a piece of cake.

PART 5
PLAID SHIRTS AND PINE TREE PANORAMAS

KIMONOS ON THE GOLF COURSE

THERE'S AN OLD BLUES refrain that goes: "I'm built for comfort; I ain't built for speed." I always thought that would make a nifty bumper sticker. Come to think of it, it would make a good tattoo for me—given my personal corporeal silhouette.

I wish it applied to clothes. Have you noticed how clothing styles seem more and more to be built for speed? Or something— they sure aren't built for comfort. Consider jackets. I've only got two that I actually enjoy wearing. One is an ancient, olive-drab battle jacket from, I believe, the Spanish army. My other favourite is an indestructible Harris tweed that weighs in at about twenty-six pounds and stands in the closet all by itself. No hanger necessary.

Well, you can see right away that the perimeters of my social life are severely restricted. There are not that many formal, or even semi-formal, occasions at which you can show up dressed in an aging Spanish army battle jacket. The Harris tweed is a problem too. Very warm. It's advisable never to wear the tweed in temperatures that exceed about 55° Fahrenheit ... unless you enjoy looking like you're sitting in a sauna.

Then too, people tend to act a little silly when you show up in a Harris tweed with leather elbow patches. It brings out the heckler in even close friends. They tend to greet you with cries of, "Oh I say, Pip Pip old chap!" Or, "Driving the MG today, are we" Where's the meerschaum?" Things like that.

I got to musing about my jackets, and about clothes in general

174

and the comfort factor in particular because of a gift I got for Christmas. It's a kimono. I don't mean one of your Hugh Hefner burgundy sateen numbers with a felt playmate on the breast. This is an authentic Japanese kimono—the kind Richard Chamberlain padded around in, in the movie *Shogun*. With the huge billowing sleeves and the wide "obi," or belt. And you know something? This kimono is the most comfortable thing I have ever worn. No buttons ... no zippers ... nothing to ride up or fall down. Wearing a kimono is like walking around in the nude. Better! Because I'm warm and not likely to be arrested for indecent exposure.

It appears I'm not the only one who's discovered the virtues of the Japanese kimono. You know where you just might see a lot of them this spring? On the golf course. No, really!

A lady by the name of Shizue Takizawa says the kimono is the perfect costume for golfers—especially for those who overswing. And she should know. She's president of the Takizawa Kimono Academy in Tokyo. She says the cylindrical shape of the garment keeps the feet together and that the "obi," tied tight over the hips, keeps the torso from—over torquing, if you will.

And the arms. Ho ho! Shizue Takizawa doesn't talk about the arms but take it from me, the arms of a traditional Japanese kimono are so capacious and unrestricting that it would be a cinch to swing a club with them. Heck, you could carry your whole club bag up one of those arms!

There are only two problems with my kimono. One of them is that ... well, I don't live in downtown Tokyo. In these parts, once you get more than fifteen or twenty feet from your own bedroom, people look at you a little funny if you're dressed in a kimono. You don't see grain handlers down at the docks dressed in kimonos. Why I bet I could count on one hand the number of lumberjacks who wear kimonos on the job.

The other problem with the traditional kimonos? No pockets! Where do traditional Japanese folks carry their car keys and grocery lists and balled up lottery tickets? Search me. Or search them, I guess.

I can think of a solution to the "no pockets" problem ... but I don't have the courage to try it. It would be audacious enough for me to walk into a Canadian bar wearing my kimono. If I had to open my purse to pay for the beer I'm not sure I'd ever be heard from again.

No, when all is said and done, I'd be happy to come to any social function you'd care to invite me to. But if I can't wear a Harris tweed or a Spanish army battle jacket then I'm sorry ... that's the night I always wash my hair.

U.S.–SOVIET INTERPLANETARY POSSE

HE'S DONE IT AGAIN. The man who once dismissed the whole environmental movement, saying: "Wellll, if you've seen one redwood you've seen them all."—has performed the same service for peace. Ronald Reagan has told some Maryland high school students that during the Geneva Summit talks, he assured Gorbachev their two countries would unite forces—if ever Earth is attacked by aliens from outer space.

That's good news. This is the same president who once kibbitzed about commencing bombing in five minutes! Nice to know a door is opening, albeit an intergalactic one.

Besides, I have this letter from a friend of mine who lives in the bush of Northwestern Ontario. She had a bear problem too. For the last few weeks they've had this big black bear showing up in their yard. He was getting bolder and bolder and she was getting scared. Almost as scared as her two watchdogs which cowered under the front porch whenever the bear showed up.

The dogs were useless and my friend has three little kids—she couldn't take chances. They had to get down the old .303 and shoot the bear.

She writes that the moment that bear hit the ground, those dogs came out from under the porch like a pair of four-footed Ninjas. Took the best part of a week to skin and dress the bear and during that week the dogs never stopped barking and snarling.

"Sure is comforting," she writes, "to know that we are safe from dead bears in the yard."

177

Which puts me in mind of the U.S.–Soviet interplanetary posse President Reagan seems to visualize. He's saying we can have peace in our time right after a war of the worlds, that we could get rid of the threat of nuclear war, if we could just persuade Martians to invade.

Dunno what it all proves. Maybe it proves the old maxim that every nation gets the government it deserves ... and any nation that elects a B movie actor gets to live in a B movie.

Speaking of actors ... where's Orson Welles when you *really* need him?

THE LOVER'S BENCH

L ET ME TELL YOU ABOUT a threesome you won't see in the park every day. It's a ten-foot long, one-ton heavy bronze sculpture now living in the lobby of New York's Penta Hotel. It is called The Lover's Bench . . . for two out of three obvious reasons (two of the three nudes are embracing) . . . and it has been around. It started public life in front of a downtown Toronto shopping arcade that caters to the Carriage Trade. The Carriage Trade took one look at The Lover's Bench, uttered a collective "EEEEEK!"— and The Lover's Bench was on the road, bound for more congenial surroundings where they appreciate this sort of thing.

Such as Montreal, where the sculpture lived on public display for six years, before murmurs of "mon dieu" and "Qu'est-ce que c'est" began to coalesce into a groundswell. Luckily, art collector Abe Herschfeld happened along about then. Abe liked what he saw, bought it and moved it south of the border. He later agreed to display the work in the lobby of the Penta Hotel, and that's where The Lover's Bench stayed.

Until a busload of southern Baptists holding reservations showed up at the front desk, expressing a whole different set of reservations—not to mention an ultimatum: get rid of The Lovers Bench they said, or they would find themselves another hotel.

That's not the sort of thing hotel managers wish to hear from entire busloads of guests—especially ones that pack their own Gideons. The Penta Hotel came up with a compromise.

They didn't run the The Lover's Bench out of town the way Toronto did. They didn't flog it to foreign interests as did Montreal. Nope, New York covered the The Lover's Bench ... with a red sheet.

It's a standoff. The owner, Abe Herschfeld wants to take it back ... Penta Hotel management is saying let's not be hasty ... and to complicate matters, the city of Montreal is making conciliatory noises along the line of "all is forgiven, please come home."

I figure there are really only two face-saving options. They can call in that European artist, Cristo, who specializes in bagging islands and buildings and Parisian bridges in acres of plastic ... offer him a small commissioned project. Or they could sell The Lover's Bench back to Toronto.

Hey, that wouldn't be so tough! Toronto may not know much about art, but it likes what it knows. All they'd have to do is change the name from The Lover's Bench to the New Domed Stadium ... featuring a fully retractable red sheet.

JE SUIS MARXISTE—
TENDENCE GROUCHO

I'VE BEEN THINKING ABOUT A problem that we don't suffer much from in Canada, this being such a polite nation and all—but which has beset and bedevilled other areas of the world, notably Australia, Brazil, and the New York subway system. Graffiti, I'm talking about. Comes from the Italian word *graffito*, which means "a scratching." It's a word that was first applied to wall scribblings found around Pompeii and other Italian cities. They were the work—as is often the case today—of ancient schoolkids, vagrants, layabouts, and other assorted side-walk types whose creative urge was stronger than their sense of public decorum.

Graffiti come in different forms. Sometimes it's a witty saying. I saw one once on a wall in London that read: "God is not dead. He is alive and working on a much less ambitious project."

But sometimes graffiti are much more abstract—a stylized signature maybe, or symbol. That's the way it seems to be on New York subway cars, which are covered with what look like Martian memoranda along the lines of *Arco 693* or *Barzak*. Of course in the case of New York graffiti artists, they're working under duress. They use spray cans on a speeding canvas and then only when the subway cops' backs are turned. Not the kind of conditions that contribute to pithy and erudite epigrams.

I've never been to Australia or to Rio de Janeiro, but apparently the graffiti artists thrive there, too. Although Australia and Rio are fighting back. Matter of fact they both claim to have the graffiti problem licked. In Rio they've done it with a device called the Chalk-o-drome. The Chalk-o-drome is a giant, mobile, four-sided chalk board that appears every morning at nine o'clock in one part or another of the city. Citizens are invited to slash away. They can write their names, valentines, poetry, religious messages, political diatribes ... whatever they like. The Chalk-o-drome is the city fathers' counter-attack against the hordes of graffiti artists who have been spray-painting messages on Rio's walls and public monuments at an alarming rate.

Does it work? Well, they say it does—but what else is a politician going to say if they've got a giant four-sided blackboard on wheels paid for with taxpayers' money?

Down in Australia, another graffiti counter-attack. A company there claims to have come up with a new product it calls Graffiti Gobbler. It's a cleanser they say works on walls, furniture, bricks and steel. Its inventors say it can handle everything from ink and paint to chewing gum and blood. It's pricey mind you—about fifty dollars a gallon—but I would imagine even a used Chalk-o-drome would set you back a lot more than that.

Personally, I think the chances of wiping out graffiti are right up there with a cure for baldness, human levitation and peace in our time. As for government-subsidized chalkboards ... that misses the whole point of graffiti—which is rebellion. To leave your indelible mark in defiance of established authority. To expect graffiti artists to do their work in chalk on sanctioned blackboards is sort of like insisting the Ghenghis Khan wear a tie.

Besides, graffiti can be kind of interesting. Delightful even. I ran into one on a washroom wall in Vancouver that I'd love to use on a fanatic some day. It read: "I'm afraid my karma just ran over your dogma." And my philosophical favourite bloomed on a wall in Paris during the student riots of the 60s. "Je suis Marxiste," it read, "Tendence Groucho"—I am a Marxist, Groucho variety.

As for the New York subway kind which is not usually witty—or indeed even comprehensible, all I can say is, imagine a New York subway car *without* the graffiti. Dirty, bland and boring. Graffiti artists in New York shouldn't get hasseled ... they should get public service commendations for giving the poor, harassed, subway riders something fresh to look at.

THE SIMPLE, SKILL-TESTING QUESTION

OKAY. PENCIL AND PAPER READY? Here's a simple, skill-testing question for you. Multiply 228 by 21, add 10,824, divide the result by 12 and then subtract 1,121 from that. Got it? Two hundred and twenty-eight times 21; plus 10,824; divide by 12; minus 1,121.

A simple, skill-testing question, right? Not for this furrowed brow, it ain't. For me, 7 plus 13 is a simple, skill-testing question. Anything more complicated than that, and you can talk to my accountant. Or my twelve-year-old.

But, be that as it may, that little poser I just put to you was the so-called simple, skill-testing question that a Windsor Ontario contestant was required to answer last month. Imagine. This guy picked up his phone one morning, confirmed that he was who he was, and learned that he was talking to the official Quizmaster for a nation-wide Canada Trust contest. Could he please, queried the Quizmaster, activate his ballpoint and multiply 228 by 21, add 10,824, divide by 12 and subtract 1,121. Because if he could, he would win a $50,000 condominium in Florida on the Gulf of Mexico. Hurry along now, and heh heh, no pocket calculators please.

The guy got it wrong. Is that surprising? Imagine the pressure! I mean if I picked up my phone some morning to find a Quizmaster purring that all that stood between me and a big ticket walk-up on the Gulf of Mexico was, say ... my ability to recall my middle name, I'd probably have to put the guy on hold and ring up my mother on the other line.

I think it's safe to say that most of us aren't all that good at math—even during periods of serenity with a pot of tea and goldfinches burbling in the lilacs. Talking to a stranger on the phone with a time limit and your retirement Valhalla riding on the outcome? Not likely.

I keep thinking of this poor unnamed Windsor contestant who up until last month was bumbling along, minding his own business ... maybe looking forward to a seventy-five-dollar Christmas bonus. Probably forgot he'd even entered the Canada Trust contest. Then, BOOM, a Bell telephone lightning bolt ... visions of his own private condo, endless sunsets with long walks under swaying palms, listening to the slurping surf ... all just a simple, skill-testing question away. Merely for multiplying 228 by 21, adding 10,824, dividing the result by 12 and subtracting 1,121. Let's see ... two eights ... sixteen ... carrying one ... one five six one two ... divide by twelve ... okay ... three six ... that's zero right ... oh! I've got it! I've got it, the answer is ... three hundred and six!

Pause.

"We're very sorry, sir. That's not the correct answer."

The Quizmaster hangs up. The officials go on to the next entry. Some guy in Toronto does the math correctly, and winds up with the condo. I still see that Windsor contestant, still standing by his phone, receiver hooked under his chin, double-checking his computational scribbles that run off the paper and on down the hall plaster.

Which is the main reason I steer clear of lotteries, draws, bingos, raffles, pools, and sweepstakes. Nothing lofty about it. I just know I'd blow the simple, skill-testing question.

Such as the aforementioned. Have you worked it out? The correct answer is 180. I know. I phoned Canada Trust. Then I double-checked with my accountant.

I had to do all that because when I tried it on my own, the answer I got was 7.39652 repeater.

And I even cheated with a pocket calculator.

SCRAPYARD BAIT

I T WAS SHAMEFUL. Humiliating. They took me out like big Larry Robinson hipchecking a daydreaming forward. Like a great tawny lion hauling down a crippled old wildebeest. There I was, jouncing along at the wheel, well within the speed limit. Piloting my vehicle judiciously between the white line and the curb. Obeying traffic signs, not kneecapping pedestrians, clipping Pomeranians, or menacing fellow knights of the road. And suddenly in my rear view mirror, FLAM FLAM FLAM!—an eruption of red flashing lights, a peremptory barooooooorah from a police siren. Nailed. Hog-tied. Pulled over.

I always intend to be dignified and withering in situations like that. Given the choice, I'd prefer to come across as a kind of blend of Noel Coward and Humphrey Bogart—with maybe just a suggestion of Conan the Barbarian. Friends tell me my performance under stress is decidedly Hollywoodian all right ... but tending toward a hybrid Woody Allen/Rodney Dangerfield mix.

In any case, it's hard to look truly haughty when the cops have the notebooks out and they're looming over you as you sit behind the steering wheel of a fifteen-year-old, sagging, listing, clunker festooned with rust blotches and enough scrapes, dings, dents and abrasions to qualify as a war relic. Franco-Prussian.

My vehicle is—was, I guess—a 1969 Volvo, nominally dark green. It has 124,000 miles on the odometer, but that's misleading because the odometer and the speedometer ceased to function at least four prime ministers ago. On the dashboard, what hasn't stopped working has simply fallen off. There are, I think, no original knobs on the dash anymore ... no, I take that back. The choke knob is factory-issue, but that too, is academic because my choke choked up and died six or eight years back.

All of this was running through my mind as I looked up at the police officers. I decided to go for haughty anyway. I sprang from the car, deftly slamming the door behind me, wincing as another half pound or so of corroded undercarriage tinkled on to the pavement.

"What's the problem, officers?"

They treated the question as rhetorical. The younger one was looking at me with an expression that I like to think held a certain amount of reverence.

"How do you keep it running?" he asked. I could see that they weren't going to fall for haughty, so we compromised. I begged wheedled and pleaded, while they gave me a piece of paper saying that I must bring my car in for an official safety inspection within a week. "Or," smirked the younger cop, "you can just show up with the licence plates."

Meaning, no matter how you cut it, the end of the road for my car—for there is no way this side of a many-thousand-dollar face, body and soul lift that Volvo 142 Serial Number 1423441107872 Vintage 1969 would ever pass the most lackadaisical road test, let alone one sponsored by the somber, incorruptible, no-nonsense minions of the provincial Ministry of Transportation and Communications.

But it isn't fair, dammit! Oh sure, my car is a little rusty around the edges. Oh all right, *very* rusty around the edges. Okay, okay ... it doesn't even have edges any more. But it has heart! I go slogging out there and on a cold winter morning, twist the key and ... before you know it ... she's turning over. Usually. More often than not ... pretty well.

That car wants to go (all things being equal and provided it doesn't overheat or flood or stall). And here it is, being hauled off the road. Scrapyard bait.

Hah, scrapyard! Don't talk to me about scrapyards. I called four of them. (Not that I would ever ... but just ...) I asked them, how much can I get for a feisty 69 Volvo that needs a ... fair bit of body work?

Their answers ranged from a high of "Forty bucks." to a low of "We wouldn't take it on a bet." I'm quoting.

It's not right. A car like mine deserves respect. It oughtta go out like Northern Dancer. I'd like to see my Volvo standing at stud in some upscale used car lot.

Which is why I'm going on about it right now, I guess. This is like one of those homey, hand-written notices you see on the supermarket bulletin board? Free kittens to a good home?

That's what I'm after. Anybody out there who can offer a few square feet of a back lot to an aging, even crumbling, but still magnificent auto. I don't think you should think about driving it, or even repairing it ... but it wouldn't make a half bad chicken coop ... or geranium planter ... or maybe just a piece of art trouvé. We're talking concepts here. If you qualify, you can have my old and slightly arthritic car absolutely free. Just come and take it away.

One other proviso. Given the state of my car's health, I think I'd better restrict this offer to listeners who live on my block. The downhill side.

EARTH ON THE BRINK?

ANYONE OUT THERE REMEMBER Environmental Armageddon? It wasn't very many years ago that the apocalyptic writing was on the ecological wall. Not to mention in newspapers, magazines, and on radio and TV. And the news the writing brought us wasn't good. Some dotty governor down in California by the name of Ronald something or other was horrifying nature lovers with bland little homilies like, "Weeelll ... if you've seen one redwood you've seen them all." Our forests were on the brink. Our Great Lakes too. In fact as I recall, one of them —Erie—it was ... was already dead! Oh yes. I remember the pronouncement. That was the same year all Whole Earthers added the word eutrophication to their cocktail vocabulary.

And whooping cranes. Whooping cranes were something our children would only see in zoos, if not in nature books. Wild whooping cranes were down to the last dozen and a half or so.

Even the beaver, symbol of our country, was threatened, we were told. Overhunted, made homeless by the encroachment of mindless human development. Mortally stricken by suburban sprawl, beavers too, were on the brink.

And all of this—forests and lakes and whooping cranes and beavers—all of this was just a very few years ago. The sixties ... the early seventies. Strange.

I think it is safe to say that there is no overwhelming evidence that since then, our planet management techniques have gotten noticeably better. Quite the opposite, actually. And yet look at what has happened to all of the aforementioned. Lake Erie lives. A recent report indicates that the lake that was supposed to be beyond resuscitation is, in fact, in better shape than it has been for years. Not Olympic material perhaps ... but off the critical list and getting better.

The whooping cranes are on an upward roll. Eighty-one of them recently arrived at their traditional winter nesting grounds on the Gulf of Mexico. That's the biggest flock to survive the rugged two-thousand-mile migration from Canada since biologists began keeping records on them.

And the beaver? Hah. The beaver these days is called many things, but endangered isn't one of them.

There was a time, of course, when the beaver was amazingly un-endangered. Back when the white man first arrived. The eighteenth-century explorer, David Thompson, noted in his diary, "Previous to the discovery of Canada ... this continent may be said to have been in the possession of two distinct races: Man and the Beaver." Well, he was right. The first fur traders could hunt the beaver with mere sticks, they were so plentiful. We all know from our history classes what happened after that. Human beings did what human beings always seem to do when confronted with a seemingly limitless supply of bounty ... they set out to prove that it wasn't so limitless at all. We did it to the buffalo. We did it to the dodo and the passenger pigeon and we almost did it to the beaver too—but not quite.

Somewhere along the line we stopped to catch our breath and wise legislators stepped in and slapped some legal protection on the harassed beaver.

That was a few years back. The beaver has taken advantage of the respite. Recently a report out of Saskatchewan indicated that, in the northern part of the province, the beaver are not only un-endangered, they're a positive pain in the neck. They are damming creeks. They are blocking culverts. They are washing out roads and flooding pasture land. Beaver are such a problem that landowners in northern Saskatchewan are allowed to shoot them on sight, without a permit. They are such a problem that one Saskatchewanian, John Mulhern, says disgustedly: "The beaver is simply a rodent—just like a rat." And John Mulhern is a Saskatchewan wildlife official.

Well, I think it's good news that the beaver is once again a pest. Just as it's good news that Lake Erie is rallying and the whooping crane is on the comeback trail.

As for our forests ... well, it's true that the man who once said: "See one redwood you've seen them all" went on to become leader of the western world. But it's also true that over in England right now one Mr. Hugh Batchelor of Kent is facing a jail sentence. His crime: cutting down trees on his own property. Mr. Batchelor is a big-time farmer—four-thousand acres—in Kent, who was, some years ago, lumbered by the court with an order not to cut down protected trees on his property. He ignored the court, cut down trees, and now faces a jail sentence.

Some years ago the philosopher, Buckminster Fuller, observed: "There is one outstanding fact regarding Spaceship Earth; and that is that no instruction book came with it."

But every once in a while there seem to be signs that we're working out a few of the rules on our own.

LASER TECHNOLOGY IN A CIGARETTE FILTER

I GOT ANOTHER ONE for my collection! Found it nestled in the middle of an issue of *Woman's Day* magazine, of all places. It's definitely a keeper. A two-page, full-colour spread paid for by the Lorillard Tobacco Company. It's an advertisement for a brand of cigarettes called True. The headline, in huge black letters reads: TASTE VICTORY! Sounds like a drive for war bonds, but it's not. What it is, is a classic addition to my tobacco ad collection. Why? Because of the next line in the ad copy, that's why. In only slightly less than Cecil B. de Millian type, that line announces: "Laser Technology Victorious in Cracking Taste Barrier!"

Isn't that great? Laser technology in a cigarette filter! Human scientific endeavour hasn't scrabbled this high on the slippery slopes of earthly accomplishment since Colgate's invisible shield ... or that detergent with killer enzymes that made whites look whiter clear across a corral.

Of course, I go back a ways, as far as ciggie ads go. Why, I'm so aged I can remember when a second string Hollywood ham by the name of Ronald Reagan used to grin back at me from magazines, exhorting me to smoke Camels. Or maybe it was Chesterfields. Or perhaps it was Ronald Reagan smoking Camels on a chesterfield. Or conceivably smoking chesterfields on a Camel. No ... that'd have to be Peter O'Toole. I digress!

I wanted to talk cigarette ads here—sub-species Filter Breakthroughs. Who out there remembers New Kent ... (WITH THE MICRONITE FILLLLTTERRRRRR)?

How about Double Ring Tareytons with the exclusive charcoal chamber? That one used to pull me in. I would smoke the cigarette then dissect the butt just to make sure my charcoal filter was in there, working for me.

Let's see now ... there was the recessed filter (I forget which company came up with that phenomenon). Couple of mentholated filters in there ... and, if I'm not mistaken, didn't somebody try to flog the concept that sucking in smoke through their filter was just like breathing cool mountain air? Now that's chutzpah!

And so's this. Laser technology cracking the taste barrier. You don't see that kind of brass in cigarette ads much anymore.

I guess that's not surprising. They've been a little gun-shy, the tobacco companies—what with Surgeon General reports and warnings from Health and Welfare Canada and medical condemnation after medical condemnation cutting the ground out from under them. Cigarette advertising has generally been reduced to grave, grey, tasteful, *Wall Street Journal*-ish, institutional ads of the type that liquor companies lean toward around New Year's and Grey Cup time.

But laser technology. Nope, I don't think the nicotine barons have been this adventurous since their feminist phase. Remember that? The you've-come-a-long-way-baby series featuring can-do looking women clad in overalls and welder's helmets, piloting hot-air balloons or repairing the transmission on their Porsches? —all the while dangling cigarettes off their lips? I always liked the implicit assumption in those ads that, now that women had fought and won their place in the workforce, it was time to go for true equality—particularly in the neglected fields of heart and lung disease statistics.

I wonder what the ultimate cigarette ad would be? The one that would make the tobacco company executives run down the street clad only in a bathtowel shouting "Eureka" or whatever tobacco execs yell when they're excited.

Probably it would be the announcement of a truly healthy cigarette. Sort of along the lines of this story that actually came over the wire recently. It reads: "Officials in China say they have found a way to combat the evils of smoking with a cigarette that's actually good for you. The new smoke was six years in the making and consists of a blend of medicinal herbs. The new product has not been put on the market yet, but it has been tested among senior Chinese officials who are said to have given it their approval."

Yeah. Well. Hah hah. If I was an Occidental tobacco entrepreneur, I wouldn't jump on this one too quickly. Not without a taste test. Herbal cigarettes aren't that new. You can still buy them at selected health food stores.

Go do that. And light one. I think you will agree that neither charcoal chambers nor micronite miracles nor all the laser technology in the Vulcan brainpan of Mr. Spock could crack that particular taste barrier.

Herbal cigarettes are ... "Close," as the saying goes, "but no cigar."

YOU CAN'T LOSE IF YOU DON'T BUY A TICKET

I KNOW THERE ARE a lot of people across the country right now who are not really paying attention to what I'm writing. That's because they're dreaming. Dreaming as they finger the little talisman in their pocket. Not a very impressive-looking talisman. It looks something like a subway transfer or maybe an IGA cash register slip. It's got Lotto 649 printed on the top of it. It's got their magic ticket number at the bottom.

I've been throwing myself at Lotto 649 lineups for two weeks now. Not trying to join them—just trying to get through to the other side of the mall.

It's nuts. All these people publicly announcing that they want to play a new game. They don't want to play the old one anymore. The one with mortgages and car payments and cost-of-living bonuses and job promotions. They want to play the new one. The one where you lay down a buck and pick up ten million.

Some U.S. psychologist came up with a good name for it. He calls it the mailbox mentality. He says an awful lot of people have put their lives into a holding pattern, while they wait for The Letter. They unconsciously believe that one day—tomorrow probably—they're going to open their mailbox to find a letter that reads: "Congratulations. You have just been made King of the World."

I don't buy lottery tickets anymore. I used to, years ago. We have one in this province called Wintario. It's a weekly draw. Every Thursday night the Wintario crew led by two fugitives from an Amway commercial fetch up in some Ontario hamlet's town hall or recreation centre. They smile a lot, and draw a whole bunch of numbered balls out of a machine ... and somebody somewhere wins a hundred thousand dollars. But I noticed a recurring theme in these draws, back when I was buying tickets. It was never *me*. I noticed another thing too. I noticed that on Fridays, the morning after I once more didn't win a fortune—I was in a bad mood. And so were a lot of people I worked with. Now I didn't do any controlled sociological study on this, but I got the unmistakable impression that we were all in bad moods because none of us thought we should be at work that Friday morning. We were supposed to be sipping a planters punch at the Honolulu Hilton, or butting cigars on the bank manager's desk blotter or consulting our broker. But we were not supposed to be at work at the same dumb old job we'd been on the day before.

So I didn't stop buying lottery tickets because of the cost. I stopped because the lottery tickets were sucking me into a dream world into which my chances of getting were slim.

Slim! You want to talk odds? Jimmy the Greek, a guy who makes his living as an oddsmaker, gave Barry Goldwater a thousand to one chance of beating Lyndon Johnson for the U.S. presidency. Same thing in the Nixon-McGovern contest. Sure enough, Goldwater and McGovern got carpet-bombed. But they did have one chance in a thousand.

You know what the odds are against anyone winning ten million in the Lotto 649? For their buck they get one chance in a hundred and thirty-five point seven *million* to win the pot.

But of course it isn't Jimmy the Greeks who are waiting four hours in Lotto 649 lineups. It isn't professional gamblers who are skimming ten or twenty bucks off the rent to buy a fist full of fantasy. No, it's folks like—well, there's a guy right here in my town who's invested four hundred dollars in Lotto 649 tickets. He's got it all figured out. He's gonna keep a million for himself and give the rest to the needy. I know this guy. He hasn't got four hundred bucks to play. And what he doesn't know yet is—he's not gonna win. Probably what he's going to do is watch Hockey Night In Canada tonight, drink a little too much beer. And feel like punching a wall without exactly knowing why.

They've got a great Orwellian rationale, the folks who flog

lottery tickets on my TV. Some pert and cheery bright-eyed little thing pops onto my screen and chirrups, "Remember . . . you can't win if you don't buy a ticket." If there were any teeth in our truth-in-advertising legislation, they'd be forced to amend that to: "You can't *lose* if you don't buy a ticket."

But maybe I'm all wet. Maybe there's somebody sitting out there right now whose ticket number composed of the first half of their driver's licence and the digits of their great aunt's birthday— is going to make them ten million dollars richer this afternoon. Maybe. But I wouldn't bet on it. And neither would Jimmy the Greek.

A TALE OF TWO OSCARS

THERE'S A STORY ABOUT the Irish wit, Oscar Wilde, on his first trip to North America. When he hit U.S. customs, he was asked if he had anything to declare.

"Only my genius," said Wilde.

The story doesn't say how many hours Wilde spent in the customs shed for that crack.

Going through customs is one of those passages in life during which you should never try to be funny. You know that. I know that. And John Zaritsky knows that.

Remember John Zaritsky? You might, if you watched the Academy Awards a few years back. He's the Canadian who won an Oscar for best documentary film back in 1983.

Zaritsky was riding high after the flight back from Hollywood that night. Suddenly he was a famous Canadian. An international star. His fellow passengers had toasted him with champagne, there was a little golden statuette nestled among the socks in his suitcase ... and here he was at Canada customs, coming home. Hail the conquering hero.

The customs officer asked him if he had anything to declare.

"Just an Oscar," said Zaritsky smugly.

"Value of object?" queried the customs man, who had obviously missed the Academy Awards.

Zaritsky was taken aback. He said something like: "Well ... I don't know ... It's just a little gold stat..."

"GOLD?" demanded the customs man, gimlet eyes widening.

About then, Zaritsky sensed that he was in trouble. How much was this gold statuette worth, the customs man wanted to know.

Good question. Oscars are only gold-plated, but winning one is worth millions to an up-and-coming actor or filmmaker. So how to judge its "monetary value"?

Several millions?

Incalculable?

Then Zaritsky remembered that he had signed a pledge when he won his Oscar, promising never to sell his award for more than ten dollars.

"Ahh ... it's monetary value is ten dollars," Zaritsky told the customs man.

"Is that ten dollars American, or ten dollars Canadian?" the customs man wanted to now. They settled on twelve dollars Canadian.

But it wasn't over. Zaritsky, his wife and their luggage were shepherded down to the special section. The one where all the dope smugglers and jewel thieves get sent—for the full search. Zaritsky had to face two more customs sleuths. They wanted to know exactly what percentage of the Oscar was gold and what the rest of it was made of. Where he got it. Was it a gift or a purchase...

Living in what seems to be a skit from a Monty Python movie gets tedious after awhile. Zaritsky blew his stack. He pulled a hundred dollars out of his pocket, thrust the wad at the tireless customs men and snapped: "Look, take what you need, but I have to go!"

Well, they finally worked it out. Zaritsky was eventually allowed back in his own country. Along with his twelve-dollar Oscar. If you ever get a chance to see Zaritsky's Oscar-winning film, *Just Another Missing Kid*, be sure to take it in.

It's about bureaucratic insensitivity.

A BIG HAND FOR THE LEFTIES OF THE WORLD

OKAY, QUICK NOW ... what do the following historical figures have in common?

Mandy Rice-Davies
Jack the Ripper
The Roman emperor Tiberius
Doctor Strangelove

Aside from having unsavoury characters, they all share one thing: they were left-handed.

Lefties—every one of them. Left-handed people have an unfortunate reputation, you know. And it's not just left-handedness either. You know which ear Van Gogh cut off? His left. Know which leg Captain Ahab was missing—not to mention Long John Silver? I don't even have to tell you, do I?

Left handedness is often synonymous with ridicule. Remember how Maxwell Smart answered his silly shoe phone? With his left hand. Remember which hand Charlie Chaplin carried his cane in? The left. Remember Gerald Ford, America's clumsiest president? A leftie.

Not in his politics, of course. That's one place where it really hurts to be called leftie. It's perfectly okay to say that some politician spearheads a resurgence of the right wing of the federal cabinet. But leftie? Call someone a leftie? Oh no. You don't say leftie in politics. Leftie is wild-haired, rabble-rousing bombs-and-bolsheviks territory.

But then again, you don't have to be left wing to feel ostracized by society. Being left-*handed* is enough.

It wasn't so very long ago that grade school teachers routinely rapped the knuckles of any kid they caught with a crayon in his or her left hand. I can remember a certain mother (not mine, by the way) who at dinner would snatch the spoon out of her toddler's left hand and place it firmly in the right.

I also remember the two left-handed kids on our school baseball team, trying to catch fly balls with a right-hander's mitt twisted awkwardly backwards onto their catching hand. I knew a fair number of left-handed kids ... but I never knew any who bragged about it. They all seemed to recognize that society had trouble with left-handedness.

Leftophobia. Not just an Anglo Saxon phenomenon either. Know what the French word for left is? "Gauche." The Spanish word? "Sinistro." A lot of people have had a big prejudice against the condition for a long, long time.

It's not just ignorant superstition either. There are any number of currently held medical theories about left-handedness. One of the more popular ones contends that anyone who is left-handed, is brain-damaged. That that part of the brain which governs hand control, was injured (albeit minimally) during birth.

Fortunately, that theory doesn't stack up very well against certain other "left-handed" facts. Let me give you another little quiz. What do the following people have in common?

Carl Philipp Emanuel Bach
Cole Porter
Michelangelo
Leonardo da Vinci

You guessed it. Aside from being geniuses in their respective fields, the aforementioned were all ... left-handers.

You want sportsmen? How about James J. Corbett, heavyweight boxing champ? Jimmy Connors, tennis star? Sandy Koufax, baseball pitcher ... or how about the sultan of swat—the great Babe Ruth? Lefties, all.

Entertainers? Well, there's Charlie Chaplin, Olivia de Havilland, Judy Garland, Betty Grable, Rex Harrison, Danny Kaye,

Harpo Marx, Kim Novak and Paul McCartney, to name a few.

Nope, lefties are definitely a minority, and they're definitely discriminated against. Try to buy a car with a left-handed gearshift . . . or ask Ma Bell for a left-handed telephone. But whatever they are—lefties are no slouches.

So whaddya say, Canada? How about a hand . . . a big hand—for the left-handers of the world?

You hear that?

It's the sound of one hand clapping.

I feel just like Gerald Ford.

NOLALU AND OTHER STRANGE PLACE NAMES

THERE ARE A LOT of wonderful stories about geographical place names and how they came to be—many of them from flat out misunderstanding. Canada for instance ... it's probably a corruption of an old Huron-Iroquois word "kanatta," which means collection of huts.

Similarly, Mexico's Yucatan peninsula got its name because Spanish explorers didn't understand what the natives were telling them. "Yec a tanh" was the phrase they kept hearing. They thought it was the name of the place. It was actually a Mayan phrase meaning "I can't understand what you're saying."

But you don't have to go all the way to the Caribbean to find strange place names. You don't even have to leave Ontario. Is there another province that can boast a Punkeydoodles Corners? We have one—just twelve miles from Stratford.

We even got a brand new strangely named town not long ago, based on a pronouncement by our then prime minister. Remember when Trudeau promised federal assistance for people who found themselves living in "*Dire Straits*"? Didn't take one enterprising Ontario community long to haul down the signs on the outskirts of town and replace them with placards reading "Welcome to Dire Straits, Ontario."

I grew up surrounded by small hamlets with Dickensian names. Places like Thistletown and Pottageville—even a place called Snowball.

When I moved to Northwestern Ontario it was like stumbling into Tutankhamen's tomb of wonderful monickers. Classical references. We have the town of Marathon up there. We also have an Espanola cheek by jowl with a Spanish.

In the north we pay homage to poets—the town of Dryden.

We commemorate optimism—Fort Hope.

We recognize the importance of intellectualism—Savant Lake.

We venerate and immortalize everything from the colour spectrum to the human body. Colours? Red Lake, White River, Sandy Lake, Vermilion Bay. And the body? Hah. You've forgotten Armstrong, Ear Falls? The Lake-head?

As for internationalism—we're practically a United Nations, in the great Northwest. French names—Lac de Milles Lac, Longlac, Lac Seul...

A wealth of Cree and Ojibway names—Atikokan, Kakabeka, Shebandowan, Nakina ... Attawapiskat.

And Finnish names abound—Lappe, Suomi, Sistonens Corners ... Kivikoski...

As a matter of fact it was a Finnish name that attracted me when I moved there from Southern Ontario. When I first arrived, I lived in a tiny community named Nolalu. I admit it. I was at least partially romanced into it by the sweet, birdlike lilting Finnish name. Nolalu ... isn't it lovely?

On my second summer up here, I went for a canoe trip through an area known by another of my favourite ethnic names, Quetico Provincial Park. Quetico ... Ojibway, I thought. Possibly Cree.

My stern paddler on that trip was a veteran Nolalu-ite and third-generation Finn I'd come to know and like very much. I remember that trip in Quetico. It was in Burchell Lake that I half-turned to him between strokes and said, "Tell me, Charlie, what does Nolalu mean in Finnish?" Finns—even third-generation ones—do not over-use the language. His answer was: "Nothin'."

"Nothing? What do you mean, nothing?"

"Nothin'. It's not Finnish."

"Well," I asked him, "what is it?"

"Nolalu?" he said. "S'what they used to stamp on the bottom of the logs they took out there. Nolalu—Northern Lake and Lumber."

Before the trip was over, Charlie disabused me of another

Byronic notion. The Quetico Provincial Park is not Cree. It isn't Ojibway either. Or even Finnish.

It, too, is an acronym.

For Quebec Timber Company.

I tell ya. Northwestern Ontario is a great levelling ground for romantics.

BALD AND PROUD

S OONER OR LATER ALMOST every radio broadcaster must face his personal moment of truth. Mine came at the open house held by the CBC Radio program, "Fresh Air," in the spring of 1983. I had to walk out on a stage in the Cabbagetown studio and face an auditorium full of faithful "Fresh Air" listeners, 99 percent of whom had never seen me before.

Well it was really heartening to see all you folks who turned up on a Saturday morning in Toronto, but to tell you the truth, I'm a little bit sorry it happened.

See, working on the radio is a ... strange ... way to make a living. You spend most of your working hours in a goldfish bowl of a studio with a pair of earmuffs on your head ... talking into what looks like an armour-clad ice-cream cone.

There is no one in the room with you. You're wearing earmuffs. You're talking to an ice-cream cone.

People have done long stretches in institutions with quilted walls wearing jackets that button up the back, for a lot less than that.

The thing about radio is, you can talk and talk and talk into that microphone ... but you have no real proof that anyone, anywhere is listening.

That's the unreal and slightly disconcerting side of radio, but there's another side to it. A radio broadcaster can't see his audience. But on the plus side of the ledger, the audience can't see the broadcaster.

205

For whole years at a time I can hide behind my microphone nattering away ... I don't have to wear a tie ... my socks needn't match ... I could do the whole thing in my pajamas. (I think New Year's Day I did do it in my pajamas.) And no one is the wiser.

And then something like this Fresh Air Open House comes along and spoils everything. You're able to see me. And I don't look anything like you thought I'd look. I'm older or younger; I'm fatter or I'm shorter, seedier or frumpier than you thought I'd be.

But most of all, I'm *balder* than you thought I'd be. People just always assume that people they've never met will have a full head of hair. Don't know why. Something like 68 percent of all males experience severe erosion of the hairline long before they get their old age pension. I see a respectable pattern of unadorned pates before me in the audience. Ex-prime minister Trudeau, notwithstanding a few heroic and overworked wisps, is bald. Julius Caesar was bald. Well, perhaps I shouldn't pursue that particular line of reasoning.

No, the thing about being bald is, it's not really *good* for anything. Little boys, when they grow up, want to be cowboys or firemen or Mounties. They never plan on being bald. There's no glamour or money in it.

But it has its advantages, being bald. Less bathroom time for one thing. My father, who was balder than I am, used to comb his hair with a damp washcloth.

On the other hand, all the young athletes in the locker room at my handball court are developing hernias from the hair dryers they have to haul around. Can't go out of the locker room without fluffing and teasing and strafing their hair with long whining bursts of hot screaming air until it's as dry as a patch of Arizona scrub pine.

Needless to say, I invariably beat them to the bar.

You save more than time by being bald. I get very few certificates of appreciation from shareholders in Brylcream, thanking me for my continued support. I don't much worry about whether my shampoo is full-bodied, extra rich, vitaminized, ultra-organic or ph balanced.

If I find small white drifts on my shoulders I know I'm in the middle of a snowstorm, not a dandruff attack.

Most of all, being bald is a tremendously liberating experience. It frees you from worry. Worry about going bald. You *are* bald. You don't have to think about it anymore, and you can take it from there.

Unfortunately, male vanity being the awesome force it is, a lot of baldies take it to their friendly neighbourhood rugmaker. They shell out several hundred dollars for a toupee or a hairpiece, and that's a big mistake, I think. Frank Sinatra wears a toupee. Burt Reynolds wears a toupee and everybody *knows* Frank Sinatra and Burt Reynolds wear toupees. So why bother?

And even if you spent thousands and got the ultimate toupee, I'm convinced that *I'd* never be convinced. I'd always worry that it was slipping or that the colour didn't match, or the price tag was showing. In other people's eyes I'd always read that haunting Clairol refrain: "Does he or doesn't he ... only his hairdresser knows for sure..." Who needs it?

Hair transplants? No thanks. Anytime I'm tempted to, pay for the thrill of having divots of hair yanked from my chest and slammed into my scalp I'll think about Bobby Hull. He had a hair transplant a few years ago. Had it all done in one weekend, between games. You're not supposed to have it done in one weekend. Bobby Hull came out of it with blackened eyes, a swollen nose and looking altogether like he'd been mugged by the entire first line of the Philadelphia Flyers. His eyes and nose look fine now, but the hair that grows on Bobby Hull's head looks exactly like the hair that ought to be growing on Bobby Hull's chest. When Bobby Hull comes on my TV to sell me a can of motor oil, I have the uncomfortable feeling that I'm being addressed by a man with alfalfa sprouts on his head.

Naw, transplants aren't the answer. Toupees aren't the answer. So what is the answer? Well, the answer is to learn to live with it. Baldness I mean. More than that—to rejoice in it.

It's time for us skinheads to come out of the closet. Be bald and proud. We obviously have nothing to hide. We'll stop talking about lack of hair. We'll call ourselves hirsutely disadvantaged. Better than that—we won't talk of going bald, we'll talk of "gaining face." Wholesale changes! Why shouldn't this very program be re-christened "Fresh Hair"?

We shall have our pantheon of hairless heroes. Sir John A. was bald. Picasso was bald. Sir Winston . . . ah . . . Sir Winston. Do you know what Lady Astor once said to Churchill? She said: "Winston, if you were my husband I should flavour your coffee with poison."

And Churchill raised that great, grizzled, bulldog-faced, bald head of his, regarded the woman sourly for a moment and replied, "Madam, if I *were* were your husband I should drink it."

I'd *shave* my head to get off a line like that.

DEBIT CARDS

WELL ARE YOU FINALLY getting used to life in a credit-card, cashless society? Too bad. Time's up. Forget credit cards. They're obsolete. What you gotta have now is your debit card. Debit cards streamline the often clumsy and time-consuming process of separating you from your money. But perhaps a brief lesson in historical high finance is in order.

There was a time (within living memory for some of us dinosaurs) that a body desirous of owning, say a Mark Seven Frassleheimer, went about it thusly. First, the body would work for a while, for which the body would receive a paycheque. One took one's paycheque to the bank which would trade one cash for the paycheque. One then took the fistful of cash to the nearest Frazzleheimer franchise and handed it over to the toothily grinning man in the loud plaid blazer.

The next wrinkle was chequing accounts. Writing cheques cut down the trips to the bank, not to mention eliminating the hazards of walking from bank to Frazzleheimer dealership with a handful of cash. But it was still clumsy. The invention of credit cards fixed that. A credit card says, in effect: give me one of those pink Frazzleheimers because the people who gave me this card are willing to wager that I'll live long enough to pay for it—even at 24 percent interest.

Better . . . but still a lot of paperwork. The Frazzleheimer dealer has to type up the details of the deal and send it to Charge Card Central. Folks there have to be notified so they in turn can send you your bill, to be followed by a series of Dear Deadbeat letters. Still too clumsy and time consuming.

Debit cards do away with all of that. With this innovation, all you do is hand the debit card to your friendly Frazzleheimer salesman. He puts the card in one of those Star Warsy computer terminals ... and, providing you're not on the lam financially, Presto, Zappo! The money is electronically transferred from *your* bank account to the *Frazzleheimer* bank account.

Or so they claim. I'm from the old school that stoutly resists the concept that money can be transferred *anywhere* electronically. Money isn't like that. Money is palpable. Sometimes it jingles, the better kind crackles ... but it's there. Some folks keep it crisp and wrinkle-free in elkhide billfolds, others wad it up in a ball and stuff it in their Levis. I've seen twenties that look too clean to be legit. I've seen five spots sporting grocery lists, telephone numbers and a Groucho Marx mustache ball-point-penned onto Laurier's unamused visage. That's what money is like. It's real. You can hold it in your hand. It does not transfer electronically. Numbers! *Numbers* transfer electronically!

Why, I was down at my bank only the other day ... just me and a serpentine chain of 138 other customers watching the final moments of our lunch hour trickle away while we waited for the bank computer to perform its various and meaningful numerical transactions.

Couldn't. Wouldn't. As the aptly named "teller" told us all, "The computer is down."

Down where? I wondered. Down in Vegas, I'll bet, with its little teflon elbows propped on the green felt in front of the five-card stud dealer. Doubtless drawing to an inside straight. With my money.

Well, they say widespread use of the debit card is still a good three to five years away and I say thank Mammon for that. That gives me a half a decade at the outside to take a crash course in Low Finance and actually learn to understand things like charge cards, PCAs and how a company can charge citizens 24 percent interest and still stay out of police custody. Or I could use that three- to five-year lead time to pursue option two: An intensive study of North American native culture with particular emphasis on the revival of an ancient craft. How to make Wampum—the last form of currency I truly understand.

Money. Mystery writer Ross MacDonald said it all. "The trouble with money," said Ross, "is that it costs too much."

THE BOOK OF FAILURES

THE SUBJECT FOR DISCUSSION today is failure, as exemplified in hoary old axioms like: "If at first you don't succeed, try, try again"; and "Winners never quit, while quitters never win"; also "Defeat does not rest lightly on these shoulders."

That final quote is taken from the dressing-room wall of the Toronto Maple Leafs, who each season, in a hockey league of twenty-one teams, manage to finish perilously close to twenty-first. Which reminds us that all bromides should be taken with a grain of salt.

My favourite observation concerning failure comes from a wag by the name of Bill Vaughan, who expresses his philosophy thusly: "In the game of life it's a good idea to have a few early losses, which relieves you of the pressure of trying to maintain an undefeated season."

My sentiments exactly. The strain of being perfect all the time is just too damned hard on a body—which explains why most of us learn to abandon all hope of a no-hitter in the very early innings of life.

The problem with failure is that it can become habit-forming. Ask the Toronto Maple Leafs. You put together a string of six or eight screw-ups in a row and you get to thinking that maybe this is the way the rest of your life is going to go—a drunken meander from disaster to disaster.

Is that the way you've been feeling about yourself of late? Well, take heart. Doctor Black has just the nostrum for that kind of negative thinking. It's an antitoxin in the form of a paperback called *The Book of Failures*. As the editor, Stephen Pile, explains in the preface: "Success is overrated. Everyone craves it despite daily proof that man's real genius lies in quite the opposite direction. Incompetence is what we are good at—it is the quality that marks us off from animals and we should learn to revere it."

Well, "revere," I dunno ... but this book will at least help you to laugh at mankind's uncanny knack of botching everything he turns his thumbs to. The book will also make you feel lots better about your own mundane foulups. You will learn that in the crap game called life you are a fringe player at best. Lots of folks have messed up, 'way worse than you.

Take the world's noisiest burglar for instance. He was a Frenchman who, in 1933, attempted to rob the home of a Parisian antique dealer. The burglar (who gets full marks for flair) attempted the job while dressed in a suit of fifteenth-century armour. Awakened by an ominous clanking, the homeowner spied a suit of armour ascending his stairs. He pushed it over, dropped a chest of drawers across the recumbent figure and summoned the gendarmes. The police were ... curious. "Why the suit of armour?" they asked the suit of armour. A thin voice from deep inside explained, "I thought it would frighten him."

It didn't. What's more, the weight of the chest of drawers put a serious crimp in the breastplate so that the burglar had to spend another twenty-four hours inside, during which time he had to be fed through the visor.

From suits of armour to chariots of tin: did you have trouble passing your driver's test? Then take comfort from the sad tale of Miriam Hargrave of Wakefield, Yorkshire. Mrs. Hargrave is the not-so-proud holder of the world record for driving test failures. Between 1962 and 1970, Mrs. Hargrave took 212 individual driving lessons. During that period she also tried her driver's test. Thirty-nine times. On the third of August, 1970, Mrs. Hargrave tried for the fortieth time and—to the dismay of fellow motorists and the delight of Wakefield Body Shop owners—passed.

One final story, also in the automotive vein. We all know too well that winter is on the way and we all know even better that some frigid morning this winter we are going to struggle out to our car, fumble the key into the door lock and . . .

Nothing. The key is not going to budge. Frozen lock.

Well, things could be worse. Ask Peter Rowlands, the world's least successful car lock defroster. One winter morning back in 1979 Mr. Rowlands, who lives in Lancaster, England, found himself faced with a frozen car door lock. Since they don't sell much lock de-icer in Lancaster, Mr. Rowlands was thrown on his own resources. He decided that he would blow some warm air into the lock with his mouth.

We all know what happened to Mr. Rowlands.

The next passer-by saw a man kneeling inexplicably in the snow beside a car, seemingly . . . kissing . . . the door lock.

"Are you all right?" inquired the passer-by.

"Alra? Igmmlptk vrok nnngyrk!" explained Mr. Rowlands. The passer-by fled.

Luckily, Mr. Rowlands's predicament only lasted about twenty minutes. By that time his hot breath had warmed the lock sufficiently to free his lips.

All I can say is Peter Rowlands is fortunate he didn't try that trick on a northern Ontario winter morning.

He would have been necking with that car door 'til April.

The Incomplete Book of Failures, compiled by Stephen Pile, published by E. P. Dutton (1979), $4:95.

PUT UP A
PARKING
LOT

ANYBODY ELSE OUT THERE who's got a home town that really, technically *isn't* their home town? I don't know how common the condition is, but that's the way it is for me. I was born in downtown Toronto, went to public school in Etobicoke, spent most of my teenage years on the outskirts of Toronto, lived in Montreal for a while, lived in Spain and England for three years, moved back to Toronto, spent ten years in Thunder Bay ... but Fergus, Ontario is my home town. No question about it. And I don't quite know why.

Fergus is a quiet little town of six thousand or so that sits on the banks of the Grand River, about eighty miles north and west of Toronto. It's Celtic with a vengeance—the town symbol is a Scotch thistle. They hold highland games there every summer.

The town seems to have a curious magnetic effect on the Blacks —my family, I mean. My grandfather lived and worked and built some of the buildings in Fergus. Then my father's generation moved away—to the big city mostly. The old how-ya-gonna-keep-em-down-on-the-farm syndrome. But the next generation—a lot of them anyway, moved back to Fergus, and now the place is crawling with my uncles and aunts, cousins and nephews and nieces. Far as Fergus is concerned, the Blacks are sort of like the Scotch thistle. Easy to grow, hard to get rid of and they keep coming back. Me, I only spent one high school year and a lot of summers in Fergus. But it was enough. Fergus is my home town.

Well, all that garrulous preamble to get around to the observation that Fergus was in the news not long ago. Made the wire service when they tore the Fergus Town Hall down.

Let me tell you about the Fergus Town Hall, since you'll never get to see it. It was one of those big, old limestone buildings. You know the kind? Sat smack on the banks of the Grand River, right in the downtown heart of Fergus. Big, square grey blocks looked like they'd last forever. Well, the Fergus Town Hall lasted 115 years ... and *then* they had to knock it down. Saw quite a bit of Canadian history, that town hall. The local militia used to meet there to drill when the Fenians were the I.R.A. of Upper Canada. Sir John A. Macdonald spoke there once. Oh it was a fine sturdy, thoroughly Southern Ontario Scottish building, the town hall. And some people recognized it as such. The Ontario Heritage Foundation pledged $25,000 for its restoration. Fergus Town Council put up $35,000 to keep it intact. Heck, senior citizens raised $60,000 to keep the Fergus Town Hall standing. But they all failed. The Fergus Town Hall was owned by the Melville United Church next door. And the United Church had plans for the land the town hall stood on.

Funny how it sticks in my mind though ... that old town hall. A lot more beautiful buildings have gone under the wrecker's ball. Canadians are especially adept at "modifying" their architectural heritage. That's why much of our country looks like the outskirts of Hoboken, New Jersey.

Maybe this bugs me because this has happened in Fergus before. Some years back they took down the Royal Bank in Fergus. Now that wasn't Notre Dame Cathedral either—but it was ... charming. It was made out of local stone by local hands—including my grandfather's. It had a tower on it. I think it's safe to say there was no other Royal Bank like it in the country. But it was hard to heat they said, so they levelled it, and replaced it with one of those modern, featureless, all-purpose buildings—could be a McDonalds in Brandon, a Texaco station in Truro or a change house on Coney Island. Happens to be the Royal Bank—Fergus branch. Looks like a cheese box on a raft.

I'm glad I wasn't in Fergus when they knocked the town hall down. There were a lot of sad and angry people there. Some of them held candles when the crane moved in. One old man stood and cried when the wrecking ball took its first swipe at the front

215

wall. Somebody asked the demolition crew foreman if he thought the town hall was structurally unsound. He replied, "I think I would have to lie if I said there was anything wrong with those walls."

That was an understatement. It took the massive wrecking ball eleven shuddering swings before a single stone fell to the ground.

Ah well, you can't stop progress, eh? That's what they say. And Melville United Church did need the space. Did I mention why they had to knock down the town hall? Despite petitions from town council and the Heritage Foundation and senior citizens?

For a parking lot. The place where the Fergus Town Hall stood for 115 years . . . is now the Melville United Church parking lot.

A GIANT FLIP FOR BURGERKIND

THEN THERE WAS THAT magic moment in 1987. A small step for man; a giant flip for burgerkind...

Here is what we know. We know that it will happen soon. Late this month, probably. We know that it will happen in one of thirty-one countries. We know that it will happen under a pair of plastic golden arches. And we know that it will sound approximately like this:

Plop.

That is the sound of one beef patty ... flipping. A historic beef patty in this case ... on its way to a rendezvous with another all-beef patty, special sauce, lettuce, cheese, pickle, onion on a sesame seed bun.

United, they will form McDonald's fifty *billionth* burger.

Fifty billion!

Do you have any idea how many burgers fifty billion is? It is one hamburger for every human being who has ever lived! Cro-Magnons, Aristotle, Madame Benoit ... the works! Fifty billion hamburgers is *ten* Big Macs for every man, woman and child *currently alive*—with enough left over to throw one helluva barbecue party.

And it all goes back to an autumn afternoon in 1948. Harry Truman is president. The world is safe for democracy ... and a fellow by the name of McDonald is plopping a hamburger on a grill in a drive-in restaurant in San Bernardino, California.

That was McBurger number one. Now, after thirty-six solid

years of committing ground beef to heat, McDonald's is closing in on McBurger number fifty billion.

Whoever gets that fifty billionth burger is going to be one famous McCustomer.

Which means it won't be me. I'm not a lucky guy.

Nope. If I was lined up at McDonalds . . . and the guy in front of me got Big Mac number 49 billion, 999 million, 999 thousand, 999 . . . and I stepped forward and the McWaitress singsonged "YES SIR?" and the back room was all a-tingle with press photographers and TV crews and high level McBureaucrats with crate loads of prizes and awards and lifetime McVouchers . . . all waiting for me to place my order and win instant fame. . .

I'd probably ask for an Egg McMuffin.

THE HORRID
OLD HAG
ON THE HUMBER

MAGICAL MYSTERY TOUR TIME, folks ... bit of a Canadian history quiz. I'm gonna read some descriptions of a certain spot in Canada. Your job is to guess what Canadian place I'm talking about. Okay?

Here's how one Edward A. Talbot described this place, way back in 1824: "The situation of the town is very unhealthy, for it stands on low, marshy land, which is better calculated for a frog pond or beaver meadow than for the residence of human beings."

Here's another observer—Anna Jameson—describing the same place in 1828: "It is like a fourth or fifth rate town with the pretensions of a capital city."

And nearly a century later—in 1923—Aleister Crowley saw the place this way: "As a city, it carries out the idea of Canada as a country. It is a calculated crime against the aspirations of the soul and the affections of the heart."

I'm afraid the impressions didn't improve with age. In 1940, author Wyndham Lewis called it "a mournful Scottish version of America." In 1941, a visiting physicist, Leopold Infeld, wrote wistfully: "It must be good to die here. The transition between life and death would be continuous, painless and scarcely noticeable in this silent town."

In 1960, the Irish playwright Brendan Behan opined that: "It will be a foin town ... when it is finished."

Well, if you haven't figured out what Canadian town I'm talking

219

about by now, then you must be a Russian spy. And not a well-briefed one at that. It's Toronto of course. Nasty old Hogtown. The metropolis Canadians love to hate. As Lister Sinclair once said: Hating Toronto is the one thing Canadians agree on.

Toronto's been getting bad reviews since the days when it wasn't even Toronto yet. The British had the city of York; the Americans had New York. We got Muddy York.

For long generations French Canadians regaled themselves with Toronto swipes. The archetypal Toronto joke: "First prize: one week in Toronto. Second prize: two weeks in Toronto. Third prize: three weeks in Toronto." Har har har.

Yup, Canadians have had a lot of rib tickling and back slapping at Toronto's expense ... for quite literally, hundreds of years. Right up until about five or ten years ago. You notice that hardly anybody's laughing about Toronto anymore?

It kind of trickled out to a hollow chuckle sometime there in the mid-seventies. About the time when you found that you could pick up a copy of a large American newspaper, turn to the travel section and find a two-page, full-colour spread extolling the glories of ... Toronto?

Yeah, somewhere in the mid-seventies Americans (well, American travel agents anyway) embarked on a full-scale hearts and flowers love affair with our old Hogtown. "It's clean!" they marvelled; "It's safe!" they crowed. "It speaks English!" And of course it was right in the backyard and offered a juicy rate of exchange on the buck to boot.

It's odd. After two hundred years of being the Rodney Dangerfield of North American communities, Toronto is finally getting some respect. It figures, when you think of it. Other North American cities are burning up from riots or falling down from urban blight or just glumly filing for bankruptcy. And Toronto, unaccountably, just keeps getting better and better.

And just recently, the chairman of the Metro Toronto Board of Police Commissioners announced that crimewise Toronto is now, per capita, the safest city on the continent. And it's not just safe. It's time to hurl ourselves against the walls of heresy and admit out loud, in public, on the air ... that Toronto is ... interesting. Yes! Any community that can have Morley Callaghan and Harold Ballard co-existing within a few city blocks of each other has to be downright intriguing—if not fascinating.

Nope. Jokes about Toronto are now as outré as Polish jokes or Newfie Jokes. The horrid old hag on the Humber has turned into a really quite ravishing, jet-setting *ingénue*.

The question is: if Canadians don't have Toronto to kick around anymore—what in the world will hold this country together?

Not to worry. There's always Ottawa.

BANNING
BALDNESS
CURES

THE TROUBLE WITH THE USFDA, y'know, is that it has absolutely no sense of humour. The initials stand for the United States Food and Drug Administration. It's a kind of a panzer division of steely-eyed bureaucrats, part of whose mandate is to keep close tabs on all the commercial substances Americans are putting on and in and around themselves. The USFDA rides herd on everything from bubble gum to Shredded Wheat; from corn plasters to Q-tips.

Which is fine with me. I mean, Canada peeps over the USFDA's shoulder, taking notes, then tells us what we frostbacks can and can't ingest, inject, inhale, and slather over our carcasses.

I'm all for that. I'm glad someone is keeping track of all the gunk charlatans and shysters try to sell us during the breaks of "Hockey Night in Canada." But I also think the FDA watchdogs have to keep a sense of proportion. Last week they announced plans to ban baldness cures. No more lotions, creams or other non-prescription products that claim to grow hair or prevent hair loss.

C'mon, you guys! That's going too far! Speaking as a card-carrying chrome dome, I think you are out of your depth, and way off base to boot.

This ban is going to do for hair restorers what the FBI did for marijuana. Once upon a time marijuana was a silly barnyard weed. Catnip for cattle. Then J. Edgar Hoover decided it was a Communist plot to subvert youth. Now that it's illegal, a thimbleful of marijuana in a Baggie fetches eighty-five dollars. *And* it's probably only oregano sprayed with Quick Start.

That's what the Food and Drug Administration ferrets are going to do with their ban on hair growers. I can see it now: a black market in baldness cures. Pathetic, jittery men with red-rimmed eyes and receding hairlines prowling around unsavoury waterfront dives and haunts ... waiting for the whisper from the shadows: "HEY, MANNN ... YOU WANT UPPERS? DOWNERS? ... HAIR GROWER?"

And here's the Food and Drug Administration proposing to get rid of whole shelves full of salves, pomades, and unguents ... all under the flimsy pretext that such baldness cures ... don't cure baldness. They don't work, complains the FDA.

Well, of course they don't work! What does? Would buying a Volvo make me a thoughtful university graduate? Does drinking Chivas Regal make me wealthy and urbane? If I shaved with a Bic would that give me a McEnroe backhand? Would wearing a glitter glove turn me into a falsetto-voiced rock star?

To paraphrase Tina Turner: What's glove got to do, got to do with it?

Baldness cures aren't selling cures for baldness! They're selling hope! Just like Lotto 649 and Rex Humbard.

The difference is scale. You can spend your whole paycheque on lottery tickets and lose. Those TV evangelists will take your house and car if you let 'em.

Baldness cures run about $3.49. So it doesn't work. So you're out $3.49. C'mon, Food and Drug Administration, you've got more important things to do than harass the dream merchants who peddle hair restorer. How about those TV preachers, for example? How about nailing them for truth in advertising? Rex Humbard in particular. I'd swear on a bible that man's wearing a toupee!

POMPADOURS, LEOTARDS, AND OTHER EPONYMS

AIN'T WORDS WONDERFUL? I love 'em. I love beautiful words like phaeton and murmuring ... I love ugly words like victual and ... well, ugly's a pretty ugly word. I love weird words like snafu and bumf ... I also love a whole legion of words that ride under a banner emblazoned "eponyms."

My dictionary says an eponym is a "real or mythical person whose name is or is thought to be the source of the name of a city, country, an era, an institution or the like."

Leningrad, Washington, Prince Albert are urban evidences of eponyms. Rome takes its name from Romulus, the mythical founder supposedly raised by a she-wolf.

But eponyms don't show up just on city names. Look at our clothes. Leotards, raglan sleeves, Levis, cardigans—all take their names from real people. Folks don't wear bloomers much anymore I guess ... and pompadours are passé ... but they will perpetuate two long-dead ladies for a while yet—namely the Marquise de Pompadour and one Mrs. Amelia Bloomer.

You or your loved one sport a set of sideburns? You probably wouldn't if a nineteenth-century American military man hadn't popularized them first. His name was General Burnside. Somehow over the years the rear echelon of his name outflanked the front and burnsides became sideburns.

Food and drink have been well and thoroughly eponomized. We eat *sandwiches* today because a compulsive gambler by the name of John Montague was so obsessed with cards and dice he could spare no time for meals. He ordered his cook to just slap something between two slices of bread and leave it at his elbow.

John Montague wasn't just a gambler in a hurry. He was also an Earl. The fourth Earl of Sandwich.

Some not so nice characters in history have been eponymically immortalized, so to speak. Boycott, for instance. In the struggle between Irish peasants and absentee landlords in the 1880s, one Captain Boycott was extremely savage in his capacity as a landlord's agent. The peasants didn't have many options for retaliation ... so they just pretended that the Captain didn't exist. They "boycotted" him. Male chauvinist pigs can thank Nicholas Chauvin for the second adjective in their epithet. Monsieur Chauvin was a French military veteran who believed and acted as if the sun rose and set on Napoleon. Such fanatical and reactionary devotion became known as chauvinism.

Ever had a boss who was a martinet? Who hasn't. Well, Martinet was another French militarist. A general in the reign of Louis XIV who reformed the infantry with all the zeal of some office managers we have known.

There are other examples of eponyms—a few of them French. Nicotine ... that comes from a sixteenth-century French lexicographer by the name of Jean Nicot who sent some of the New World seed to Paris. Guillotine? Doctor Joseph Guillotine of the French Academy of Medicine was the man who first suggested the general blueprint for a machine that would efficiently cause wrongdoers to lose their heads in a manner amenable to the state.

Two of my favourite eponyms are ones that you would never suspect: Booze and Blurb.

Blurb, of course, is one of those "greatest story ever written" eulogies that appear on the covers of cheapish and sometimes not so cheapish novels. We owe that one to a Miss Belinda Blurb, who appeared on the back cover of an otherwise forgotten potboiler around the turn of the century. And Booze? Thanks to one Edwin G. Booze, a Philadelphia distiller who flogged his particular brand of rotgut so enthusiastically that clients stopped asking for whiskey and simply ordered ... Booze.

Hmmm ... Booze and Blurb ... two eponyms and they both begin with B.

Me? I'm Arthur *Black* formerly of Thunder *Bay*...

Well, you've heard of the Black Sea, haven't you?

PLAID SHIRTS AND PINE TREE PANORAMAS

WELL, CITIZEN, HOW DOES it feel to live in the Gerald Ford of nations? It is now official: Canada is Dullsville. The questionnaires have all been handed in and the results neatly tabulated, annotated, footnoted and transmogrified into percentages, bell curves and full-colour, three-dimensional graphs. No matter how you read it, it comes out the same: when the world turns its eyes on Canada, all it sees is coast-to-coast grey flannel. Our country comes across as a listless, unlettered, unlovable waif, possibly the outcome of a night of grim passion between Ed Sullivan and Eleanor Rigby. We are perceived to possess neither the flamboyance of our French maman, the stiff-upper-lippery of dear Pater, nor the raffish easygoingness of our cheeky car-salesman Big Brother next door. Nope, if nations of the world were television programs, Canada would be a test pattern.

Canada's blandness is now statistically certified, and what's especially humiliating is the fact that you and I paid for the diagnosis. It comes from a study that was commissioned by Tourism Canada. The department virtually leafletted the windshields of the world, conducting surveys in Britain and continental Europe, not to mention Australia and Japan.

"What does Canada mean to you?" the surveys asked in a plethora of tongues and a flurry of multiple-choice variations. Back came the answers in what amounted to a polyglot reprise of your average Nelson Eddy/Jeannette MacDonald movie. "We think of virgin forests and snow-capped mountains," said the

Japanese and the Australians. "We think of Mounties, French-Canadian trappers and Indian maidens in buckskin," said the West Germans, the Dutch and the French. "We think of wide-open spaces, beautiful sunsets and igloos on ice floes," said the English, the Spanish and the Belgians.

"Oh dang!" cried Tourism Canada, peevishly stamping its galoshes. Folks in the department had kind of hoped that Canada might be perceived as . . . well, hip, darn it all. You know—sort of suave and with-it—maybe even a touch awesome. Instead it's the same old story: plaid shirts and pine tree panoramas with a loon serenade in the background.

To tell the truth, I'm surprised that Tourism Canada was surprised. All the study tells us is that nothing has changed. Canada has been stereotyped as the Nerd Among Nations for years—centuries even. Voltaire dismissed us as "a few acres of snow" back in the middle of the eighteenth century. A hundred and fifty years later the English poet Rupert Brooke took the grand tour and pronounced with a sniff that our Dominion was "alive . . . but not kicking." Canada's been branded everything from a sanctimonious icebox to a bowl of vichyssoise ("cold, half-French and difficult to stir"). I once heard Lenny Bruce cop some easy laughs talking about "Canada—the place where everybody drives those old cars."

Isn't it rather bizarre that a country that routinely produces flakey fauna the like of Joey Smallwood and Harold Ballard should get stuck with the boredom rosette? Has no one been to the American midwest? Belgium? Liverpool, England?

Check out the Canadian impact on Lenny Bruce's own turf: comedy. Canada's done its bit to prod the planet's funnybone, turning out everyone from Mack Sennett (Richmond, Quebec) to David Steinberg (Winnipeg)—and not forgetting a trio that's currently hot: Martin Short (Hamilton), Dan Aykroyd (Orillia) and John Candy (Toronto).

Truth to tell, half the writers of all the comedy sitcoms in Hollywood have earmuffs on the skeletons in their closets. It just doesn't figure that a deadly dull country could produce such a disproportionate number of gagsters.

Export-wise, it seems like fantasy is Canada's forte—and not just comedy fantasy either. We've got melodrama covered—why we've supplied dream merchants from Louis B. Mayer to Monte Let's-Make-A-Deal Hall; from Perry Mason to Pa Cartwright. What's an up and coming nation gotta do to get its name on the world's dance card, anyway?

Methinks a Shakespearian cad by the name of Cassius put his lean and bony finger on the problem when he observed: "The fault, dear Brutus, lies not in the stars but in ourselves, that we are underlings." So it is with Canada. Our problem is not that we are a stone drag, but that we *think* we are. We've got a severe case of sibling envy. We are in awe of our Big Brother to the south.

One of our serious Hollywood contributions, Donald Sutherland (St. John, New Brunswick) put it this way: "... every single Canadian has a feeling that people in the United States have some kind of visceral, cultural and life experiences he does not have. If you're a Canadian you think about a person from the States as the brother who went to sea, caught the clap and made a million dollars in Costa Rica or Hong Kong."

Well, it's to be expected I suppose. The last three generations of Canadians have grown up drenched in American heroic mythology—everything from Rambo to Superman to Jack Armstrong, all-American Boy.

Remember Jack Armstrong? It was a radio adventure program back in the pre-TV days, all about a blue-eyed, blonde-haired kid who routinely made the world safe for democracy every Saturday night while impressionable kids on both sides of the border gathered around their radios to listen, slack-jawed. I was surprised to learn recently that the idea of the show was based on a real Jack Armstrong who actually did have a rather heroic life. He was a U.S.A.F. colonel, a member of the Atomic Energy Commission and one of the men responsible for launching the first U.S. nuclear-powered satellite. The real Jack Armstrong died recently in California at the age of seventy-four. What I found especially interesting was the last line in his obituary. It read: "Colonel Armstrong was born in Winnipeg, Canada in 1911."

There's more than a nugget of irony in the story of Superman as well. The Man of Steel was conceived not on the planet Krypton, but in downtown Toronto. A fellow by the name of Joe Shuster dreamed him up while toiling for the Toronto Star. In fact, in the early Superman stories, mild-mannered Clark Kent worked for the *Daily Star*, not the *Daily Planet*.

Now we have Rambo, the latest American superhero. Rambo is a Jack Armstrong/Superman for the 80s who restores America's honour and wins the Second Vietnam War all by himself. Rambo is, of course, played by Sylvester Stallone, a man who's ego is only slightly larger than his pectorals, but Rambo wasn't created by Stallone. Nope, the character comes from a book written by one David Morrell. Mr. Morrell was born and raised in . . . wait for it . . . Kitchener, Ontario. Canada.

Ahhh America. Where would you be if Canada ever turned off your fantasy pipeline?